Rethinking
the
Church

Also by James Emery White

A Search for the Spiritual
Life-Defining Moments
Long Night's Journey into Day
Embracing the Mysterious God

maudie

Rethinking the Church

A Challenge to Creative Redesign in an Age of Transition

Revised and Expanded

James Emery White

Foreword by Leighton Ford

Baker Books
A Division of Baker Book House Co
Grand Rapids, Michigan 49516

Published by Baker Books
a division of Baker Publishing Group
P.O. Box 6287, Grand Rapids, MI 49516-6287
www.bakerbooks.com

Fourth printing, November 2006

Printed in the United States of America

Library of Congress Cataloging-in-Publication Data
White, James Emery, 1961–
    Rethinking the church : a challenge to creative redesign in an age
of transition / James Emery White; foreword by Leighton Ford.—Rev.
and expanded ed.
        p.   cm.
    Includes bibliographical references.
    ISBN 10: 0-8010-9165-9 (pbk.)
    ISBN 978-0-8010-9165-0 (pbk.)
    1. Church renewal. I. Title.
BV600.2.W496 2003
262'.001'7—dc21   2003001422

Contents

Foreword

A half century ago I was a high school student in Canada with a deep concern to introduce my generation to Jesus Christ, who had become a living reality for me. Through involvement in Youth for Christ, I came to know a visionary group of young pioneers with a passion to evangelize their generation. Among them were Billy Graham, then a staff evangelist with Youth for Christ; Bob Pierce, who founded World Vision out of his heart for children; Jim Raburn, who saw America's teenagers as a vast mission field and launched Young Life; Dawson Trotman, who discipled servicemen through the Navigators; and Bill Bright, who targeted the campuses of America. Most of the young pioneers I met were men. All of them had a passion for Christ and the gospel, and they were willing to think in new ways.

I can remember late night prayer meetings at the Youth for Christ conferences at Winona Lake, Indiana, where these young men of God would lift their voices in prayer for the lost and the needy. They left an indelible imprint on my life.

Now, fifty years later, God is raising up a new generation of leaders with new visions for their world. Again, all of them have a passion. I am glad to say they include both men and women. And they are a source of great hope. Their hunger for God, their vision for the world, their fresh thinking, and their deep passion inspire me. Today I encounter these young men and women through Leighton Ford Ministries, where we are committed to raising up young leaders worldwide who will lead others to Jesus.

Jim White is one of those young leaders whom I have come to know and admire. I have watched as he has helped to give birth to a new, vibrant, and fast-growing church in our own exploding community of Charlotte, North Carolina. I have talked with him and have sensed the authenticity that comes from the way Christ has intersected the deep needs of his own life. I have been impressed by the combination of a vibrant heart, a visionary faith, and clear thinking that mark Jim's ministry. In all this he is typical of this generation of new leaders that God is raising up, not only in the United States but around the world.

But Jim also typifies this new generation of leaders in two other ways. He is not at all satisfied with "ministry as usual." He knows that after half a century of unrelenting evangelism, America is still a mission field. Indeed, the United States is now the largest mission field in the English-speaking world with over two hundred million people who have at the most a vague connection to Christ and his church. Jim knows that we need new ways to attract these people.

Jim is also a church planter. I have noticed that many of the young men and women who have a passion for evangelism believe that the planting of new churches is key to evangelizing America. Many of those who might have gone into parachurch ministries forty or fifty years ago are selecting church planting. The parachurch groups still have an essential place, but church planting is on the cutting edge of the future.

So it is important that Jim has written, out of his own experiences and heart and mind, this book, *Rethinking the Church*. "Rethinking" is a good translation for the word *repentance*, for to repent means to change our way of thinking. It is literally "after thought." Jim is helping us to rethink evangelism, discipleship, ministry, worship, community, and the structure of the church. He begins by taking us back to the source and using the early church as described in the Book of Acts as a paradigm. From this he raises important questions and points to some of the important answers.

This book is not the last word on the church. No book will be. But I pray that God will use this book to help pastors and lay leaders who are frustrated at the way things are and hopeful about the way things can be to rethink and to act in brand-new ways, led and empowered by the Spirit of God.

Leighton Ford

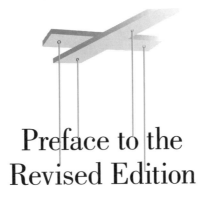

Preface to the Revised Edition

I am deeply grateful to the editors at Baker for allowing me the chance to revise and expand this work. The modifications throughout have been designed to enhance the ongoing vitality and relevance of this work to bring about thoughtful approaches to change. The distinctives that many found helpful have hopefully been retained—namely, the book's simple, concise treatments of the key areas for rethinking and the freedom from specific models of ministry or faddish techniques that can often cloud the issues. Because of the book's uncomplicated nature, a wide range of churches and denominations have been able to use it strategically for the purposes of rethinking foundational issues related to methods and processes.

Where needed, statistics and findings have been updated so that the research on which the book was founded might continue to be vital and, if necessary, corrected. The near universal call from readers for a chapter on moving from rethinking to change has been heeded and has been added to this new edition.

Mecklenburg Community Church recently celebrated its tenth anniversary, bringing clarity to the founding vision and the principles of rethinking on which it was established. I have enjoyed incorporating a decade's worth of learning throughout this new edition.

When I first wrote this book, I thought that the most important area for rethinking revolved around process. I still hold to its importance, and it is the heart of this book. What I did not foresee was what was truly at hand, which was simply the building of a church that would flourish. *Rethinking the Church* has been used by denominations and seminaries, leadership teams and entire congregations as a way to explore creative redesign for optimum levels of ongoing effectiveness. My goal in this revision is to serve the continued ministry of this work for many more years to come.

Preface

This is not another book on church growth, future trends, or contemporary models of ministry. It is not a book that tells the success story of a particular church in order to make that church a model for others to follow. It is not a lament of the church's theological, spiritual, or numerical decline. This is a book on *rethinking*.

What is *rethinking*? It is the radical redesign of church processes for dramatic improvement in the fulfillment of the church's purposes and mission.[1] The most important word in that definition, however, is not *radical*. There is certainly a need for change in the church, but I am not one to call for change just for the sake of change. What is more important is a return to *process*, something the church has turned its back on for quite some time. By process I mean a complete end-to-end set of activities that together fulfill the purposes and mission of the church.

There is a pressing need for the church and its leaders to rethink *why* they do *what* they do the *way* that they do it. In recent years, there has been a tendency to break the church down into specialized tasks and programs and then focus on trying to improve those various tasks and programs. Rather than rethinking the church, we have become engaged in repairing the church. But the church's problem is not a task problem; it is a *process* problem. As renowned management expert Peter Drucker was often known to say, there is a great difference between increasing efficiency—which is doing things right—and effectiveness, which is doing the right things. Rethinking the church is about effectiveness. It is not about asking, "How do I do this better?" as much as it is about asking, "Why do I do it this way?" or even more foundationally, "Why do I do this at all?"

Therefore, this is not just a book for the church "professional." It is a book for everyone who is concerned about the church and is involved in the church. I hope you like it. Even more, I hope you apply it, because the church really is the hope of the world.

Acknowledgments

I would like to thank four men in particular. The first two are Rick Warren and Bill Hybels. They are the "Roger Bannisters" of the church world. Bannister was the first person to run a mile in under four minutes, a goal that people had been trying to achieve since the days of the ancient Greeks and had concluded was impossible. The year after Bannister broke the four-minute barrier, thirty-seven other runners did the same. The year after that, three hundred runners achieved what had previously been considered impossible. Now it is not unknown for every runner in a single race to run the mile in less than four minutes. Rick and Bill, you were the pioneers who blazed the trail that so many of us have followed. Both of you, in so many ways, have been incredibly generous and giving to me through your life, time, and support.

To Leighton Ford goes great love and admiration for being both mentor and friend. You have selflessly committed your life to passing on the torch to the next generation. I hope my small flame burns half as bright as yours and that I finish the race with as much integrity. Thanks, too, for writing the foreword.

Finally, to David Dockery I extend both affection and gratitude for being that rarest of finds: a good, loyal, and lasting friend. You have always supported my calling.

In addition to these four men, there are two institutions that deserve a word of thanks. Both the Moscow Theological Institute and the Southern Baptist Theological Seminary allowed me the privilege of serving as a visiting professor during 1994. Much of this book was conceived during my time on those two campuses. Being a glutton for punishment, Southern invited me back during the summer of 1996, and the final touches on this book were completed during that time.

I also wish to express my deepest love and gratitude to the family of faith known as Mecklenburg Community Church. You have chosen to believe in both me and the dream. You have given me your trust, your support, and your partnership. You have overlooked my weaknesses and celebrated my strengths. I stand in awe of you and all that you are doing for the kingdom. With you, I can know and be known, love and be loved, serve and be served, celebrate and be celebrated. You are the rethinking embodied.

And finally, I thank my wife, Susan, who continues to be the woman of my dreams. Once again, you made every page possible.

Soli Deo Gloria.

Introduction

My grandfather lived well into his nineties. Toward the end of his life, he made a comment that deeply intrigued me. He said, "Jim, I've seen the world go from the horse and buggy to the space shuttle." At the time, I was fascinated by the breadth of his life but equally challenged by the fast-paced nature of change. My grandfather witnessed nothing less than the transformation of the world. But so will you and I. More information has been generated in the last three decades alone than in the previous five millennia. Over four thousand books filled with information and knowledge are published every day. A single weekday edition of *The New York Times* includes more information than the average person in seventeenth-century England encountered over the course of his or her entire lifetime.[1] The implications of such rapid change have had an impact not only on our lives but on our institutions.

A Lesson from the Business World

For decades, most companies have operated on the basis of Adam Smith's insight that industrial work is best carried out by breaking everything down into its most basic tasks. In their landmark book *Reengineering the Corporation,* Michael Hammer and James Champy write that this set of principles "laid down more than two centuries ago has shaped the structure, management, and performance of American businesses throughout the nineteenth and twentieth centuries."[2] Yet due to the continual transformation of the world through rapid change, Hammer and Champy go on to say that "the time has come to retire those principles and to adopt a new set. The alternative is for corporate America to close its doors and go out of business."[3] Bottom line: To survive, those in the business world have to rethink how they have traditionally done business.

But proponents of change have also learned that the biggest barrier to reengineering is the past success of the institution. Observers have noted that "American companies are now performing so badly precisely because they used to perform so well."[4] In other words, a company such as IBM became successful because it was uniquely designed for the time in which it prospered. Once that context changed, however, the previous insights and processes that once brought success now guarantee failure. As a result, the problem with America's business world "is that it is entering the twenty-first century with companies designed during the nineteenth century to work well in the twentieth,"[5] and "the old ways of doing business . . . simply don't work anymore."[6]

Rethinking has not been limited to business. It has had to take place in every other sphere of our modern world. From the media to the government, education to the military, rethinking such foundational issues as structure and strategy has become absolutely necessary not merely to prosper but to survive. Yet the most important institution of all—the church—often continues to operate on insights forged in the late nineteenth and early twentieth centuries. As Leith Anderson has written, the church is literally "dying for change," and it is taking its toll.[7]

The State of the Church

Studies on church growth indicate that for the vast majority of American churches membership numbers have either plateaued or are declining. This decline began in earnest at the end of the twentieth century. For example, a twenty-year study of membership between 1965 and 1985 revealed that virtually every mainline denomination was in decline, including United Methodist (-16 percent), Episcopal (-20 percent), Presbyterian (-24 percent), and Disciples of Christ (-42 percent).[8] More recent figures have not altered this portrait, with the Presbyterian Church (U.S.A.) losing close to 100,000 members in 1995 alone, and the United Church of Christ and the Christian Church (Disciples of Christ) combining for another 50,000 members lost.[9] According to the latest report from a series of ten-year studies conducted at the same time as the U.S. Census, this stunning decline of mainline churches is comprehensive and shows no sign of ending. From 1990 to 2000, the United Church of Christ lost almost 15 percent of its members, the Presbyterian Church (U.S.A.) 11.6 percent, the United Methodist Church 6.7 percent, the Episcopal Church 5.3 percent, and the Evangelical Lutheran Church in America 2.2 percent—all while the U.S. population increased by 13 percent.[10]

Figures from the Southern Baptist Convention—easily one of the more evangelistic Christian denominations—while growing to 20 million at the end of the 1990s, also reveal that nearly 70 percent of all Southern Baptist churches are either plateaued or declining, with overall growth well below the pace of U.S. population growth.[11] Even the 20 million figure is misleading, for as Thom Rainer, dean of the Billy Graham School of Missions, Evangelism and Church Growth at the Southern Baptist Theological Seminary, has noted, 4 million of those haven't joined the church. Another 8 million are nowhere to be found. Only around 8 million of the 20 million are actually in church on any given week.[12]

The Southern Baptists are far from alone. When investigations into the number of plateaued or declining churches is broadened to include all Protestant churches in the United States, the figure leaps to 80 to 85 percent.[13] British demographer David Barrett notes that now more than 53,000 people leave church every week, never to return.[14] The result? Just one out of every six Protestant churches (17 percent) has 200 or more adults attending its services on a weekend, with average attendance in the mainline Protestant churches—United Methodist, Evangelical Lutheran, Episcopal, Presbyterian Church (U.S.A.), and United Church of Christ—dropping to just 98 adults.[15] Indeed, half of the congregations studied in the *Faith Communities in the United States Today* report, the largest survey of congregations ever conducted in the United States to date, which began to release its findings in 2001, have fewer than 100 regularly participating adults. A full quarter of congregations has fewer than 50 regularly participating adults.[16] Barna's research shows a staggering 10 percent drop in the average number of adults attending services at a Protestant church between 1997 and 2001 alone.[17]

Rumors of a mid-decade revival during the 1990s, supposedly counteracting these declines, were premature. In January 1996, the Barna Research Group found that within the week prior to being polled, only 37 percent of Americans attended a worship service. The polling firm noted that this was the first time the percentage of attendees had dipped below 40 percent and the lowest recorded level of attendance among Americans since the firm began tracking religious involvement in 1986.[18] Equally mistaken were those who believed there would be a post–September 11th rise in attendance. After a momentary spike, figures settled into earlier patterns. The *Wall Street Journal* likened it to "the CNN effect" in television. "When calamity strikes, viewers tune in and ratings soar. Then when the smoke clears, they click the remote and ratings fall off."[19] During a typical week in 2002, no more than 42 percent of Americans were present at a church service.[20] Current data also shows that the proportion of adults who can be considered unchurched has grown substantially since the early 1990s. In 1991, just 24 percent of all adults were unchurched; in 2002, 34 percent fit that description.[21] The *World Christian Encyclopedia* estimates that worldwide there are more than 112.7 million unchurched adults, with expectations of that number doubling by 2025.[22]

Listening to the Unchurched

Why the decline? Many would be tempted to believe that it is due to the increasingly secular nature of our postmodern world. While there can be little doubt that this is a factor, it is not the reason the unchurched give for their disenfranchised state. In preparation for planting Mecklenburg Community Church in Charlotte, North Carolina, I commissioned a survey of unchurched people who live in the northeast area of Charlotte.[23] The heart of the survey sought to answer a single question: Why don't you attend church? Those being surveyed were allowed to cite as many reasons as they felt applied. Here are the results.

1. *There is no value in attending.* The number one reason people give for not going to church is that there is no value in attending. These people feel they can connect with God just as easily, if not more so, on the golf course as they can at a weekend church service. Church doesn't do anything for them, and they don't get anything out of it, so why attend? While many people who do not attend church are interested in spiritual things, they do not feel that the church has very much to offer them in their spiritual pilgrimage.
2. *Churches have too many problems.* People also choose to remain outside the church because they feel churches have too many problems. The assessment of the unchurched

is that a typical church is made up of people who are inflexible, hypocritical, judgmental, and just plain mean. Division and discord are perceived to be more present in churches than in many other groups. Why would anyone want to become involved with something that, in their mind, is so obviously dysfunctional? As one man quipped, "I've got enough problems in my life. Why would I go to church and get more?"

3. *I do not have the time.* Few would argue that time has replaced money as the new currency in contemporary American society. As a result, many people claim to be unchurched because they simply do not have the time to attend. Yet people make time for the things that matter to them. Those who claim a lack of time believe they will receive little or no benefit by attending church.

4. *I am simply not interested.* People express a lack of interest as a fourth reason for not attending church. Ironically, spiritual interest in America has never been higher. Books on spiritual topics from angels to near-death experiences are runaway best-sellers. Religious issues such as the power of prayer, healing, and moral values are hot media topics. *Swing,* a magazine that targets people in their twenties, ran a headline that declared "Spirituality Returns."[24] In the article, it was noted that in a recent survey of twentysomethings, finding spiritual fulfillment was more important than achieving financial success. George Barna's research has discovered that three-quarters of all adults say it would be "very desirable" to have a "close relationship with God."[25] People are very interested in spiritual things, are asking spiritual questions, and are on spiritual quests as seekers, yet they have no interest in the church. As Robert C. Fuller has written, the largest group of unchurched people in the United States are not secular humanists but people who are deeply

spiritual, just not religious.[26] Indeed, according to the research of sociologist Wade Clark Roof, over half of all Americans have come to believe "that churches . . . have lost the real spiritual part of religion."[27] This is like having a country full of people who are deeply and passionately interested in finding and experiencing a hamburger but are driving right past McDonald's on a daily basis with nothing but indifference.

5. *Churches ask for money too frequently.* People claim they do not attend church because churches seem more interested in their money than in them as people. The unchurched perceive the church to be money driven with a continual emphasis on financial contributions. According to these people, services are better known for large, red "thermometers" gauging the success of never-ending fund drives than they are for helping people experience God.

6. *Church services are usually boring.* People also choose not to attend church because they think church services are usually boring, predictable, and lifeless. There is little within the service that captures and holds their attention.

7. *Christian churches hold no relevance for the way I live.* The seventh reason people reject church has to do with relevance. These people feel the Christian church is simply out of touch with life in the modern world. The topics, music, and language make them feel as if God

---

Reasons People Give for Not Attending Church

1. There is no value in attending. (74%)
2. Churches have too many problems. (61%)
3. I do not have the time. (48%)
4. I am simply not interested. (42%)
5. Churches ask for money too frequently. (40%)
6. Church services are usually boring. (36%)
7. Christian churches hold no relevance for the way I live. (34%)
8. I do not believe in God, or I am unsure that God exists. (12%)

---

is buried somewhere in the past or is removed from the world in which they live.

8. *I do not believe in God, or I am unsure that God exists.* The eighth and final answer is surprising: disbelief in God. Only a small percentage said they do not attend church because they have rejected God.[28]

This research indicates that most people who do not go to church do not attend for clear and specific reasons. Their problem is not with Christian theology; it is with how we do church.

Of course, the issues facing the church go well beyond a drop in attendance or an inability to connect with unchurched people. There are many indications that those who remain in the church are also frustrated by the nature and experience of their ministry involvement, a lack of effective discipleship, worship services that are not truly worshipful, and internal politics and procedures. As a woman once commented to me after I spoke at a conference, "I go to church because I feel like I have to, not because I want to. It's never really been a positive, meaningful experience."

Rethinking the Church

If people would have been asked in 1968 which nation would dominate the world in watchmaking during the 1990s and into the twenty-first century, the answer would have been uniform: Switzerland. Why? Because Switzerland had dominated the world of watchmaking for the previous sixty years.

The Swiss made the best watches in the world and were committed to constant refinement of their expertise. It was the Swiss who came forward with the minute hand and the second hand. They led the world in discovering better ways to manufacture the gears, bearings, and mainsprings of watches. They even led the way in waterproofing techniques and self-winding models. By 1968, the Swiss made 65 percent of all watches sold in the world and laid claim to as much as 90 percent of the profits.

By 1980, however, they had laid off thousands of watch-makers and controlled less than 10 percent of the world market. Their profit domination dropped to less than 20 percent. In a single three-year span, fifty thousand of the sixty-two thousand Swiss watchmakers lost their jobs. Why? The Swiss had refused to consider a new development—the Quartz movement—ironically, invented by a Swiss. Because it had no mainspring or knob, it was rejected. It was too much of a paradigm shift for them to embrace. Seiko, on the other hand, accepted it and, along with a few other companies, became the leader in the watch industry.

The lesson of the Swiss watchmakers is profound. A past that was so secure, so profitable, so dominant was destroyed by an unwillingness to consider the future. It was more than not being able to make predictions—it was an inability to rethink how they did business. Past success had blinded them to the importance of seeing the implications of the changing world and to admit that past accomplishment was no guar-antee of future success.[29]

As with the Swiss watchmakers, a set of methods and practices set down in a previous generation has shaped the ministry, evangelism, and organization of American churches throughout the twentieth century. Further, as with so many other institutions, the biggest dilemma facing the church is the past success of the church. Yet the church's very survival in recent history has been tied to its willingness and ability to adapt to the unique conditions of the day.[30] Success can only be continued through appropriate, thoughtful adjustments to our processes and methods.

Rethinking the church has nothing to do with compromis-ing the church's message. It has nothing to do with attempt-ing to provide a single model for all churches to follow. It is about individual churches, under the leadership of the Holy Spirit, grappling with Jesus' words: "You find it easy enough to forecast the weather—why can't you read the signs of the times?" (Matt. 16:3 MESSAGE). And then it's about reading those signs and coming to grips with Jesus' teaching about the nature of change: "No one tears a patch from a new garment and sews it on an old one. If he does, he will have torn the new garment, and the patch from the new will not match the old. And no one pours new wine into old wineskins. If he does, the new wine will burst the skins, the wine will run out and the wineskins will be ruined. No, new wine must be poured into new wineskins" (Luke 5:36–38).

It is time to rethink the church.

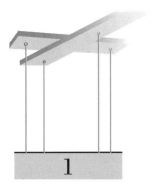

Rethinking the Foundational Questions

In the late 1800s, no business matched the financial and political dominance of the railroad. Trains dominated the transportation industry of the United States, moving both people and goods throughout the country.

Then a new discovery came along—the automobile—and incredibly, the leaders of the railroad industry did not take advantage of their unique position to participate in this transportation development. The automotive revolution was happening all around them, and they did not use their industry dominance to take hold of the opportunity. In his videotape *The Search for Excellence,* Tom Peters points out the reason: The railroad barons didn't understand what business they were in. Peters observes, "They thought they were in the train business. But, they were in fact in the transportation business. Time passed them by, as did opportunity. They couldn't see what their real purpose was."[1] They failed to ask themselves any of the foundational questions.

Introducing the Questions

A foundational question is one that penetrates to the very essence of a person, business, or organization. For the railroad industry, foundational questions would have included What business are we in? and What is the ultimate goal of all our efforts? In other words, the railroad barons needed to get at the heart of what it was they were trying to *do* through the railroads. Answering such questions would have led them to realize that they were not really in the railroad business at all. They were in the *transportation* business. Their ultimate goal was not the preservation of a particular system of transportation but transportation itself.

Ron Pobuda of the National Audiovisual Association provided a contemporary example of this same idea when he said, "If *Sports Illustrated* magazine understood it was in the sports information business, not the publishing business, we would have the Sports Illustrated Channel, not ESPN."[2] This is the power of a foundational question: It gets underneath momentary methods, tools, and fads, keeping an organization focused on its most basic identity and objective.

Rethinking the church begins with answering the foundational questions. It is not that the church has never answered them before; the church just hasn't answered them recently in light of the changing realities of our modern world. The answers have become layered beneath tradition and habit, custom and ritual, convention and routine. To rethink the church, we must get behind and underneath the methods and programs of our day and focus on what it is those methods and programs are attempting to achieve.

The Foundational Questions

- What is the purpose of the church?
- What is the church's mission?
- Whom are we trying to reach for Christ?
- What determines whether the church is alive and growing?
- How will we accomplish the mission God has given to us?

The foundational questions help individual churches remain clear about what they are fundamentally trying to do as a church. Once this is understood, then there is a foundation for creative and effective rethinking of how best to do church in the modern world.

What are the foundational questions a church needs to answer? The list could certainly be expanded, but here are five essential questions a church needs to consider on a continual basis:[3]

1. What is the purpose of the church?
2. What is the church's mission?
3. Whom are we trying to reach for Christ?
4. What determines whether the church is alive and growing?
5. How will we accomplish the mission God has given to us?

These questions get at the heart of the church, and answering them can form the basis for creative, comprehensive rethinking.

1. What Is the Purpose of the Church?

During World War II, the Nazis set up a camp factory in Hungary where prisoners were made to labor amid barbarous conditions. One day the prisoners were ordered to move a huge pile of garbage from one end of the camp to another. The next day, they were ordered to move the pile back to its original location. No reason was given—they were just told to do it.

So began a pattern. Day after day the prisoners hauled the same mountain of garbage from one end of the camp to the other. The impact on the prisoners of that mindless, meaningless labor and existence began to come to the surface. One day an elderly prisoner began sobbing uncontrollably and had to be led away. Then another man began screaming until he was beaten into silence. A third man, who had endured three years of labor in the camp, suddenly broke away and began running toward the electric fence. He was told to stop or he would be electrocuted. He didn't care. He flung himself on the fence and died in a blinding flash.

In the days that followed, dozens of prisoners went insane. Their captors were callous and indifferent, for what the prisoners didn't know was that they were part of an experiment in mental health. The Nazis wanted to determine what would happen when people were subjected to meaningless activity. They wanted to see what a life would become without a sense of purpose. They concluded that the result was insanity and suicide. The commandant even remarked that at the rate prisoners were killing themselves, there would no longer be a need to use the gas chambers.[4]

Purpose is decisive to human life. Allan Cox has written that an organization that has lost sight of its purpose has no soul.[5] To use marketplace terminology, understanding our purpose is understanding what business we are in. What is the business, or purpose, of the church? There are many passages in the Bible that give us an answer but perhaps none more clearly than the following section from the Book of Acts:

> They devoted themselves to the apostles' teaching and to the fellowship, to the breaking of bread and to prayer. Everyone was filled with awe, and many wonders and miraculous signs were done by the apostles. All the believers were together and had everything in common. Selling their possessions and goods, they gave to anyone as he had need. Every day they continued to meet together in the temple courts. They broke bread in their homes and ate together with glad and sincere hearts, praising God and enjoying the favor of all the people. And the Lord added to their number daily those who were being saved.
>
> Acts 2:42–47

30

From this passage, it is clear that the early church was devoted to the apostles' teaching—*discipleship*. The early church was devoted to fellowship—*community*. The early church was devoted to the breaking of bread, to prayer, and to meeting together in the temple courts—*worship*. The early church was devoted to meeting the needs of other people—*ministry*. Finally, the early church was devoted to church growth, particularly through conversion—*evangelism*.

These five activities—discipleship, community, worship, ministry, and evangelism—constitute the business, or purpose, of the church. It is what a biblically functioning community looks like. It is what the church does. But like the railroad, a church can forget this foundational purpose. Rather than worship or evangelism, a church can fall prey to thinking that its purpose is keeping up a tradition, holding a particular event, meeting a budget, or maintaining a building. These activities may flow *out* of a purpose, but they do not make up the purpose of the church itself.

In his book *The Purpose Driven Church*, my friend Rick Warren calls for churches to recapture their biblical sense of purpose and then to look at everything their church does through those purposes.[6] Such a move would create a climate for extremely effective rethinking, because when church members look at their church through the lens of its purposes, it enables them to know what to say yes to as well as what to say no to.

There is an old story about a lighthouse keeper who worked on a rocky stretch of coastline. Once a month he would receive a new supply of oil to keep the light burning so that ships could safely sail near the rocky coast. One night, though, a woman from the nearby village came and begged him for some of his oil to keep her family warm. Another time a father asked for some to use in his lamp. Another man needed some to lubricate a wheel. Since all the requests seemed legitimate, the lighthouse keeper tried to please everyone and grant the requests of all.

Toward the end of the month, he noticed his supply of oil was very low. Soon it was gone, and one night the light on the lighthouse went out. As a result, that evening several ships were wrecked and countless lives were lost. When the authorities investigated, the man was very apologetic. He told them he was just trying to be helpful with the oil. Their reply to his excuses, however, was simple and to the point: "You were given oil for one purpose, and one purpose only—to keep that light burning!"[7]

A church faces a similar commission. There is no end to the demands placed on a church's time and resources. As a result, the foundational purposes of a church must reign supreme. When they do, renewal flows. According to the *Faith Communities in the United States Today* report, congregations with a clear sense of purpose feel vital and alive. As opposed to feelings of unity based on heritage (the past), a purpose-driven mentality is able to look to the future.[8]

2. What Is the Church's Mission?

There is a thought-provoking scene in Lewis Carroll's classic children's tale, *Alice's Adventures in Wonderland*. Young Alice comes to a fork in the road and asks the Cheshire Cat which direction she should take. "'That depends a good deal on where you want to get to,' said the Cat.

"'I don't much care where—' said Alice.

"'Then it doesn't matter which way you go,' said the Cat."[9]

The cat's reply is insightful. Without a clear destination or goal, there can be no sense of direction, and therefore, one course of action is as good as any other. Alice had a purpose— walking. She just didn't know where her walking was supposed to take her. This is why asking the second foundational question is so important: What is the church's mission?

Think of the church's mission in military terms. It is one thing to know the purpose of a particular military unit, such as being an infantry division. It is another to know the specific "hill" the unit is trying to take. This has to do with mission. A church might understand its purposes but not know what it is trying to accomplish through those purposes. If the biblical purpose of the church involves evangelism, discipleship, ministry, worship, and community, then the mission question is simple but profound: What specific objective is the church devoted to accomplishing through those purposes? In other words, what is the church trying to do through evangelism, discipleship, ministry, worship, and community?[10]

Jesus made many statements that spoke to how he desired the various purposes of the church to come together in a singular mission. The most well known is often called the Great Commission:

> Jesus came to them and said, "All authority in heaven and on earth has been given to me. Therefore go and make disciples of all nations, baptizing them in the name of the Father and of the Son and of the Holy Spirit, and teaching them to obey everything I have commanded you."
>
> Matthew 28:18–20

According to this passage, the mission of the church is to reach out to nonbelievers and develop them, along with existing believers, into committed followers of Christ. This is the mission the purposes of the church are intending to accomplish.

Think of it in terms of a car assembly line. At the beginning of the line are the raw materials and parts needed to make a car—wire, engine, tires, chassis. As those materials move down the assembly line, a car is made, and at the end of the line, it is rolled off for service. In the same way, as people participate in the evangelism, discipleship, ministry, worship, and community of a church, activities that function under the overall mission of the church, they develop into fully devoted followers of Christ who are ready to serve him.

Yet George Hunter has observed that many churches have other missions in mind for those who walk through their doors, such as wanting people to "believe like us" doctrinally, to "behave like us" morally, to "have an experience like ours" emotionally, to "become like us" culturally, to "support the church like us" institutionally through time and money, or to "participate with us" sacramentally through baptism, confirmation, or communion.[11] These goals are not in and of themselves wrong. The problem is it would be possible to realize most of these goals within a life and still not be a Christian.[12] In other words, they have little to do with the actual mission of the church.

Church growth consultant Win Arn has observed something even more disturbing. Arn conducted a survey in which he interviewed the members of nearly one thousand churches in regard to what they perceived to be the mission of the church. Eighty-nine percent said the church exists "to take care of my family's and my needs." Only 11 percent said it existed to win the world to Christ.[13] This points to a disturbing reality: Many churches fail to have any sense of mission at all, and those that do may fall far short of having a mission that is biblical in its scope.

As a result, many churches specialize in one short segment of the assembly line. There is no effort to collect the raw material needed to build cars, and there is little effort to roll finished cars off the line for service on the road. The mission is simply a maintenance program for existing cars in which windshields are washed, fluids are checked, and tire pressure is monitored. The goal is to keep cars that have already been built well tuned and polished for the showroom.

3. Whom Are We Trying to Reach for Christ?

The power of light depends on *focus*. Light that is diffused does not make much of an impact, but if we put that light through a magnifying glass, we can set something on fire. If we concentrate and focus that light even more, it becomes a laser that will cut through sheet metal. As light becomes more powerful as it is brought into focus, so the church becomes more effective as it clearly defines whom it is trying to reach.[14]

It is common in the business world today to talk of market segmentation, niche marketing, and selective advertising. As researchers Michael Treacy and Fred Wiersema have noted, "all things to all customers" is as outdated as a manual typewriter.[15] Many congregations have wisely and appropriately taken note of this, for no single church can possibly reach out with equal effectiveness to every conceivable person. The more focused a church is on whom it is trying to reach, the more effective it will be at reaching them. Methodist strategic planner Jack Heacock says, "In the past, a lot of Methodist pastors were trying to be like the Sears Roebuck catalog, all things to all people. But in the greatest mail-order period in history, that catalog went out of business. In targeting a church's efforts, you have to get very clear on who[m] you want to try and reach."[16] It is no wonder that from the earliest days of the church, as recorded in the New Testament, it has seemed to please the Holy Spirit to birth a wide variety of churches in order to reach a wide variety of people.[17] Churches, therefore, are wise to examine such issues as geographic location, demographics, and culture.

The implications of such an understanding are far-reaching. Once a church knows whom it is trying to reach, it gains enormous insight into how to go about achieving its purposes and mission. As anyone in the marketplace will tell you, once you know who your customer is, you know *what* it is you are offering, *whom* you are offering it to, *how* you should go about offering it, and *where* you should offer it to them. Knowing whom it is you are trying to reach affects not only what you do but how you do it.[18]

Though overly simplified, there are four types of people a church can focus on reaching.[19] First, there is the churched believer, or a person who is already part of a church or is at best temporarily unchurched due to a geographic relocation. This person has already made a decision for Christ and is committed to church involvement. A second type of person a church can target is the churched nonbeliever. This is the person who attends a church but has never given his or her life to Christ. A third type is the unchurched believer. The Bible does not support the idea that one can be a committed follower of Christ and simultaneously choose not to be part of a church, yet vast numbers of such people exist. The final type of person a church might focus on is the unchurched nonbeliever. This is the person who is both outside the church and does not have a relationship with Christ.

Whom Are We Trying to Reach for Christ?

- Churched Believer
- Churched Nonbeliever
- Unchurched Believer
- Unchurched Nonbeliever

Jesus spoke clearly about the people his mission was to target: "It is not the healthy who need a doctor, but the sick. I have not come to call the righteous, but sinners" (Mark 2:17). If the mission of the church is to turn nonbelievers into fully devoted followers of Christ, then the primary target of a church should be those who are nonchurched nonbelievers.

It is not that the other three types of persons are not important or that a church should not be concerned with their well-being. The entire automotive "assembly line," as mentioned in the previous section, is important, but there needs to be a conscious understanding that the goal is to make cars. Likewise, in a church the goal is to reach people for Christ. Therefore, there is a defined target of whom it is a church is trying to reach, and that is the person who is not in a relationship with Christ.

4. What Determines Whether the Church Is Alive and Growing?

Once a church recognizes its purpose, its mission, and whom it is trying to reach, the next foundational question—one that is notoriously overlooked in the life of many churches yet is essential for rethinking—relates to the definition of *success*.

I once heard that FBI agents went into a town to investigate the work of what appeared to be a sharpshooter. They were amazed to find bull's-eyes drawn all over town that contained bullets that had penetrated the exact center of the targets. When they finally found the man who had been doing the shooting, they asked him how he had been able to shoot with such accuracy. His answer was simple. First he shot the bullet, then he went and drew the bull's-eye around where it had hit.[20]

This approach toward defining success is all too common in many churches. Whatever is happening—or not happening—in the life of a church is interpreted as a direct "hit." Sometimes mere survival is called success, or simply meeting a budget, increasing attendance, or building a building. Yet each of these "successes" can take place at the same time a church is failing in regard to its mission.

Spiritual things are inherently difficult to quantify, so many never try. Yet success for a church clearly involves fulfilling its purposes in such a way as to reach its target and complete its mission. As a result, benchmarks should be established to determine whether the mission of reaching lost people and turning them into fully devoted followers of Christ is being accomplished.

Determining Success: Part One

The first part of the mission—reaching out to lost people—can be gauged by examining the type of growth a church is experiencing. There are four primary sources for church growth:

1. *Biological growth.* Biological growth occurs when a child of existing believers with ties to a church comes to faith in Christ through his or her involvement in the church. Essentially, this is winning your own.

2. *Transfer growth.* A church can also grow through transfer growth, which takes place when a Christian moves into an area and chooses to join a church, or when a locally churched Christian makes the decision to move to another church home. Such a person does not come to a church as a nonbeliever, nor does this person come from an unchurched background. At best, he or she is temporarily unchurched due to relocation or some other life issue. This type of growth, then, results from nothing more than the movement of existing believers.

3. *Prodigal growth.* A prodigal is someone without a re-cent church background or church involvement. This person embraces Christian beliefs and, in some cases, has maintained a certain level of spirituality. For one reason or another, however, this person left the church and may have lived his or her life outside Christ's daily management and direct, personal leadership. A prodigal has certainly left the life of Christian community. Prodigal growth occurs when such a person returns to the church. Renewal and rededication may take place as part of the return and, at times, even rebaptism.[21]

4. *Conversion growth.* This type of growth occurs when a church reaches a non-Christian. Consciously or not, such a person has rejected the truth and claims of Christianity. To grow through conversion is to grow by reaching a person who has now entered into a life-changing, personal relationship with Christ as Savior and Lord.

Authentic success in regard to the first part of the mission of the church has to do with the source of a church's growth.

If a church is effective in accomplishing its mission, it will be reaching lost people. If a church is not reaching nonbelievers, then it is not being successful—no matter how well it may be doing in terms of increases in attendance, donations, and facilities.

The truth is that most churches are not successful, for the vast majority grow through transfer growth or biological growth—regardless of their number of baptisms. One of the least publicized research projects in recent years, but easily one of the most significant, discovered that more than 60 percent of adults baptized in Southern Baptist churches in 1993 had been baptized before. Further, of those who had been rebaptized, 35.8 percent were receiving their second immersion in a Southern Baptist church. Overall, rebaptisms of Southern Baptists accounted for one out of every five Southern Baptist baptisms.[22] This only supports George Barna's research, which has found that 80 percent of all church growth in America is due either to transfer growth or biological growth.[23]

Four Ways to Grow a Church

1. Biological Growth
2. Transfer Growth
3. Prodigal Growth
4. Conversion Growth

Determining Success: Part Two

The mission of the church involves not only reaching people for Christ but also developing them into fully devoted followers of Christ. Simply achieving conversions does not fulfill the biblical mission of the church. Far too many churches determine success by the number of conversions, or baptisms, or by their total church membership. This has led to a willingness to overlook the people who have their names on the rolls but who never attend church. Yet the goal is for new believers to demonstrate the marks of a Christian who is growing in spiritual maturity.

Measuring spiritual transformation is tricky at best, but there are certain characteristics present in the lives of those on the path toward true transformation that can be identified.[24] The first is a pattern of personal spiritual development and growth through a life of prayer, worship, and Bible study. Involvement in some type of small group for community, growth, and ministry is a second indicator. A third characteristic of a Christ-follower on the path toward full devotion is the discovery and use of the spiritual gift or gifts God has given this person for service. A final attribute is the management of financial resources. If Christ is present in a person's life, his or her heart will be tender and generous toward the support of the church.

If these marks are not being manifested in the lives of those being reached for Christ, then full success is not being reached, regardless of the number of people who are being converted. Success in this area has little to do with position or length of time in a church but everything to do with authentic life change.[25]

5. How Will We Accomplish the Mission God Has Given to Us?

As a young person, I played organized basketball for years. After my playing days were over, I had the opportunity to coach part time while completing seminary. Both as a player and a coach, I learned that the key to success in a game was having a strategy based on what we knew about the opposing team. The game plan was not just getting together before a game and saying, "All right, boys, let's go get 'em!" If that had been the extent of our strategy, we would have lost virtually every game.

Likewise, the final foundational question a church needs to ask has to do with strategy. How will we accomplish the mission God has given us and reach success? This is where much of the challenge of rethinking takes place, and the remainder of this book will attempt to give insight and direction for our time in light of the timeless purposes and mission of the church.

Yet much has already been done, for it is in answering the foundational questions that a church can begin to engage in rethinking. The church has a fivefold purpose, a unique and compelling mission that those purposes are to achieve, and the means by which to know if it is being successful. Now we must develop a strategy for our day in light of those timeless, foundational anchors, a strategy that begins with evangelism.

2

Rethinking Evangelism

The Chevy Nova was a relatively successful American car for many years. Encouraged by U.S. sales, Chevrolet began to market the American Nova throughout the world. Unfortunately, the Nova did not sell well in Mexico and other Latin American countries. Additional ads were ordered, marketing efforts were stepped up, but sales remained stagnant. Sales directors were baffled. The car had sold well in the American market; why wasn't it selling now? When they discovered the answer, it was rather embarrassing: In Spanish, *Nova* means "no go."[1] The business world is full of such stories. For example, when Perdue Farms, Inc., converted its popular slogan "It takes a tough man to make a tender chicken," into Spanish in hopes of expanding its chicken business, the results were less than desirable. Why? The translation was "It takes a virile man to make a chicken affectionate." Not exactly what Frank Perdue had in mind.[2]

What does this have to do with rethinking evangelism? Everything. Evangelism involves effectively communicating the gospel of Jesus Christ with the goal of converting an individual to the Christian faith. The New Testament model for evangelism is the communication of the Christian faith through contextualization, which simply means that the message of the Christian faith is to be presented in a way that makes sense to the person hearing it. Think of Jesus' evangelistic efforts. When he encountered the woman at the well, he began his conversation with the topic of water. When he encountered the fisherman Peter, his starting point was fishing. When the tax collector invited Jesus to his house, the issue of money opened the dialogue. Jesus clearly developed his presentation of God's saving message in light of the context and background of his listeners. The apostle Paul shared Christ's commitment to this approach, writing that he became "all things to all men so that by all possible means [he] might save some" (1 Cor. 9:22).

The message of the gospel is unchanging, but the method of communicating that gospel must change according to the language, culture, and background of the audience. George Bernard Shaw said that the "greatest problem of communication is the illusion that it has been accomplished."[3] This is the essence of rethinking evangelism. And as the folks at Chevrolet and Perdue Farms can tell you, failing to engage in such rethinking can be costly.

Yesterday's Evangelism and Today's Unchurched

Rethinking evangelism needs to begin with rethinking who the listeners are. We want to communicate the Christian faith to others, but who are the "others"? Picture an imaginary scale from 1 to 10. On the left end of the scale, at the 1, we have someone who is completely divorced from a relationship with or knowledge of Christ. On the other end of the scale, at the 10 mark, is that point in time when the spiritual journey of an individual results in coming to saving faith in and knowledge of Christ.[4] This is a rather crude and overly simplistic scale but one that will hopefully serve to illustrate a point.

1	2	3	4	5	6	7	8	9	10

Let's begin by using this scale to evaluate yesterday's non-believer. Speaking in broad terms, where on the scale would an unsaved person living in the United States in 1960 have been? Few would deny that the typical nonbeliever of that time more than likely had the following in his or her spiritual resume: an acceptance of the deity of Christ, a belief that truth existed and that the Bible was trustworthy, a positive image of the church and its leaders, a church background and experience that were relatively healthy, a foundational knowledge of the essential truths of the Christian faith, and a built-in sense of guilt or conviction that kicked in when he or she violated the basic tenets of the Judeo-Christian value system. So on a scale of 1 to 10, this person would have been placed at 8.

							X		
1	2	3	4	5	6	7	8	9	10

The top evangelistic strategies of 1960—door-to-door visitation, Sunday school, revivals, and busing—were well oriented to this context. For example, visitation was effective because people would open their doors to ministers and gladly invite them into their homes. Regardless of a person's spiritual convictions, failure to have done so would have been considered rude. Revivals were productive because people who needed Christ would actually attend them due to the cultural pressure to be present. Sunday school was evangelistically fruitful because individuals were not too intimidated to begin their exploration of a church through a small group experience. Sunday school enrollment campaigns also benefited from the cultural pressure to open one's door to a minister, the positive image of the church, and the built-in sense of conviction that resulted from not being involved in church. Once enrolled, there was a strong sense of duty to attend; it was, after all, the church. Bus ministries were supported by parents who would willingly allow their children to board a vehicle driven by a stranger, be transported to some building in another part of the city for a religious event to be implemented by strangers, and then be returned to them later that day. And then, because unchurched people were already at an 8 on the scale, a one-time, cold-call presentation of the gospel would be effective. After all, they did not need to move very far down the line—just from an 8 to a 10.

One of the most pressing questions for the church in today's world is this: Are the conditions and attitudes that created such a successful context for those strategies still in place today? Are the people we are trying to reach today the same as they were in 1960? The answer is no.[5] George Hunter contends that the first characteristic of a secular person in the modern world is that he or she is essentially ignorant of basic Christianity.[6] It has been said of Generation X, those born between 1963 and 1977 and the first generation to grow up in a postmodern context, that they lack even the *memory* of a hope-giving gospel.[7] Today many people outside the church struggle with the concept of Christ's deity. They think he was a good man, perhaps even a prophet, but not God in human form. Over half, in fact, believe that Jesus sinned during his lifetime.[8] Further, 72 percent of Americans now deny the existence of absolute truth, and few have confidence in the historical accuracy or ethical authority of the Bible.[9] Indeed, almost two-thirds of the adult population are dubious of the Bible's accuracy.[10] Beyond doubt is illiteracy; two-thirds of the population do not know what John 3:16 refers to, and fewer than four out of every ten Americans have any idea what the word *gospel* means.[11] Ten percent believe that the name of Noah's wife was Joan of Arc.[12]

Unchurched people of today have seen scandals erode the church's reputation and often cite negative experiences in their church background as a reason for their lack of involvement. The percentage of adults expressing confidence in religious leaders dropped from 49 percent of the population in 1974 to only 22 percent of the population in 1989.[13] Research in 1992 and 1993 found that of the four major Protestant denominations in America—Baptist, Methodist, Presbyterian, and Lutheran—none had reputations that were rated "very favorable" by even one-third of the population.[14] Further, rather than having any sense of guilt or conviction, there is a growing adherence to situational ethics. Sociologist Robert Bellah interviewed a woman named Sheila who captured the spirit of the times well: "I believe in God. I'm not a religious fanatic. I can't remember the last time I went to church. My faith has carried me a long way. It's 'Sheilaism.' Just my own little voice."[15]

But the challenge before the church runs even deeper. The average person we are trying to reach has gone through what might be called a "great divorce," meaning a separation between spiritual longing and desire and the embrace of a particular religious faith. It's not that people are far away from Christ and his church in their life and knowledge; they no longer see their spiritual desire and search as involving the discovery of a faith or religion. There are too many roads to God, so people are no longer even looking for a road. If the current malaise were simply about belief in Christianity as the "way," our challenge would be to create deeper levels of understanding. If the impasse involved doubt that Christianity is the way, we would have to make an effort to convince them. Today people reject that there even is a way, so the challenge is for the very need of Christianity itself.

Think of it this way. Any major daily newspaper has dozens of ads for new cars. But if you are not in the market for a car, you are not going to notice those ads. It doesn't matter if a dealership has a sale, promises a rebate, has a radio on-site broadcast, hangs out balloons, says they're better than everyone else, promises that they will be different and not harass you or make you bargain over the price, or sends you a brochure. If you're not in the market for a car, you're not in the market for a car. It's no different with a church. Seekers today are divorced from seeing it as a need in their life, even when they are open to and interested in spiritual things. They no longer tie their spiritual interest and longing to the need to find a particular faith, much less a particular church.

So where might the contemporary unchurched person rest on our imaginary scale? One could theorize that he or she is best placed at a 3.

		X							
1	2	3	4	5	6	7	8	9	10

If you want a biblical metaphor for the change that has taken place, think of it this way: We have switched from trying to reach out to the God-fearing Jews of Jerusalem to the pluralistic pagans of Mars Hill. And that is quite a change indeed.

Now reflect on the implications this might have on traditional evangelistic approaches. For example, it is highly doubtful in a day when reports of child molestation and sexual abuse by religious leaders make headlines and when confidence in religious leadership is so low, that many parents would allow their children to participate in a traditional bus ministry. Door-to-door visitation of any kind has been declared unlawful in many areas and impossible in the ever growing number of closed, guarded gate communities. Few people today enjoy an unannounced visitor knocking on their door and would not dare open it to a stranger. Revivals no longer have the cultural support they once enjoyed as a community event and, as a result, have very few non-Christians in attendance. Church members are finding that many people are too intimidated to begin their spiritual journey with a small group experience such as Sunday school and that traditional enrollment campaigns suffer for the same reasons as do door-to-door visitation.[16]

Even if a Christian does get in the door or gets a nonbeliever to a revival, the impact of a one-time, cold-call type of presentation is greatly diminished because the typical nonbeliever is no longer at an 8 on the scale. It takes time for someone to move down the line, and while there are a few "Saul to Paul" experiences, they are exceptions to the rule. It is time to rethink evangelism, and that begins with recapturing an understanding of evangelism as both process and event.

Evangelism as Process and Event

In my relationship with my wife, Susan, a process of dating and courtship preceded the actual event of our marriage. It is rare for people to become engaged, much less get married, on their first date. Accepting Christ is no different. When someone comes to saving faith in Christ, there is both an adoption process and an actual decision event.

For the last several decades, evangelism capitalized on a unique state of affairs, namely, a culture filled with people who were relatively advanced in their spiritual knowledge and, as a result, able to quickly and responsibly consider the event of accepting Christ as Savior and Lord. In light of today's realities, fresh attention must be paid to the *process* that leads people to the event of salvation. The goal is not simply knowing how to articulate the means of coming to Christ (the "10" moment), but how to facilitate and enable the person to progress from a 3 to the point of a 7 or an 8, where he or she is even able to consider accepting Christ in a responsible fashion.

In recent years, a personal visit from a minister or trained layperson, a revival meeting, or even a Sunday school class provided an effective setting for moving people toward Christ. Today a different setting is needed, one that is uniquely designed for the changing realities of our world.

Evangelistic Environments

When I was in elementary school, one of my teachers brought an incubator to class. We learned that an incubator maintains the kind of environment that is necessary for the birth of a baby chick. If it became too cold for the eggs, the baby bird inside the egg would die. A certain degree of warmth was needed for the egg to hatch.

When it comes to evangelism, the efforts of the church are like an incubator. Every approach, every program, every service furnishes a particular environment that will either serve the evangelistic process or hinder it. Let's use the term *seeker* to represent a person who may be open to spiritual things but is at a 3 on the scale. This person is in desperate need of someone or something to facilitate the process of moving him or her down the line toward being able to consider the event of salvation. The following types of environments are among those that a church can present to a spiritual seeker.

Seeker Hostile

The first environment a church can manifest is "seeker hostile." A church can be openly antagonistic toward seekers who might venture to attend its services.

Michelle was trapped in the demeaning world of prostitution, drug addiction, and alcoholism. Wanting to escape this life, Michelle disguised herself and hid from her pimp for several days while going through chemical withdrawal. She was discovered and dragged into the chambers of the raging pimp, where she was beaten until unconscious while the other prostitutes watched and learned. Next Michelle tried suicide—anything to escape the nightmare of her existence. A relative found her body, hours from death, and rushed her to the hospital where her life was saved.

This time Michelle turned to the only place she could imagine there might be hope—a local church. She had no sense of self-worth. Used by men, rejected by the world, she turned to God's people. She knew she deserved punishment but hoped against hope that she might find mercy. Halfway through the church service the pastor recognized her from her life on the street. Before the entire congregation he pointed her out and then lectured her for defiling the house of God with her filthy presence. Then he ordered her out.[17] An extreme case? Perhaps. But it is all too common in lesser forms.

Evangelistic Environments

- Seeker Hostile
- Seeker Indifferent
- Seeker Hopeful
- Seeker Sensitive
- Seeker Targeted

Kristina and her roommate decided to go to church because they had hit on some rough times. Kristina's roommate had become pregnant outside of marriage. They decided to search a little deeper for purpose and meaning. High on their list for investigation was Christianity.

They decided to try a church near their apartment. They went, attended faithfully, and tried to build some relationships. They both wanted to turn from the lifestyles they had been living and seek God. After just a few weeks, however, it became known in the church that the baby carried by Kristina's roommate was conceived out of wedlock. Suddenly people wouldn't sit by them and would stop talking whenever they approached. No one smiled at them when they entered the church. It wasn't long before the pastor asked them not to return because of the nature of their "situation." As you might imagine, Kristina and her roommate never wanted to darken the doorway of a church again. His explanation was simply, "You're just not our type."[18]

Seeker Indifferent

A second environment might be termed "seeker indifferent." This church climate is not hostile toward non-Christian guests, merely apathetic. The questions, concerns, and exploration process of a person who may be at a 3 on the scale and interested in moving toward a 10 are simply overlooked.

While in New England for a speaking engagement, I met a pastor of a Baptist church who shared his frustrations regarding the growth of his church. I asked him what he thought the problem was, and he responded, "Well, there just aren't any more Baptists in my area!" Cultivating an atmosphere for someone who was not a Baptist, much less a Christian, had never entered his mind. He was not hostile to non-Christians, just oblivious to them.

Seeker Hopeful

A church that creates a "seeker hopeful" environment wants to see seekers come and meet Christ, but they have never thought about the nature of the church's climate. Altar calls are extended with great hope and fervor, revivals are held, Sunday school campaigns are enacted, but the warmth of the incubator has not been adjusted. The internal environment has not been changed for years, and as a result, nothing has been done that will effectively bring in seekers, much less serve their pilgrimage toward Christ. This type of environment is like a fishing expedition in which people put bait on a hook, place it in the middle of the boat's deck, and then join hands to pray for the fish to jump in and get on the hook.

Seeker Sensitive

A fourth environment that a church can offer is called "seeker sensitive." This atmosphere exhibits some concrete efforts to draw and encourage the seeker. While the overall orientation of the church is still directed toward the growth and maturation of the "already convinced," the thermostat has clearly been adjusted to allow for eggs to receive some of the warmth and care they need in order to hatch.[19]

Seeker Targeted

The final atmospheric category is best termed "seeker targeted," a term to be preferred over seeker "driven," which would mistakenly intimate that the whim of the seeker is what determines the theology and direction of the church. In truth, a seeker-targeted environment is one in which church members place a high priority on the needs of the seeker and make every effort to remove any and every barrier that might impede the seeking process.[20] Seeker-targeted climates are just that—targeted on facilitating the process of evangelizing seekers.[21] The growth and maturation of believers is certainly cared for, but there is a conscious attempt to be an evangelistic incubator that is set at just the right temperature in regard to the front door, or entry points, of the church.

Few churches are seeker hostile in terms of their climate, but even fewer are truly seeker targeted or even seeker sensitive. The vast majority are either seeker indifferent or seeker hopeful. In today's climate, indifference and hope will not make much of an impact.

Evangelism That Works

In his research, George Barna has recently discovered that there are three reasons why non-Christians fail to be influenced by the message of Christianity. First, they do not see the relevance of the Christian faith. Second, they do not understand what it is the Christian faith is trying to say. Third, they have difficulty accepting how different the Christian answer is from what they thought the answer would be.[22] Evangelism that works actively invites people into an experience that helps them seek and then find a redemptive relationship with God through Christ. But as Barna's research has revealed, the experience will have to be relevant and understandable, because only then can the nonbelievers begin to grapple with

Christianity's radical claims. There are countless ways this can be achieved, but the key is to begin where people are and then to make the message as clear and compelling as possible. How this specifically manifests itself is limited only to the direction and creativity of the Holy Spirit, but three steps are absolutely essential.

Step One: Bridge Building

The first step that is absolutely essential in bringing someone to Christ is the building of a relationship between a believer and a nonbeliever. The typical nonbeliever is divorced from the church and, as a result, divorced from relationships with those who are within the church. Nonbelievers don't watch Christian television or listen to Christian radio. They don't read tracts left in bathrooms or attend crusades. They are effectively insulated and isolated from the Christian message. The only way they will be reached is through a relationship. Interestingly, the unchurched say the same thing. In Barna's research on Charlotte, North Carolina, mentioned in the introduction, another question asked of the unchurched was this: What would encourage you to attend a church? The results set out in the following graph are intriguing.

Net Scores for Methods of Attracting People to Church

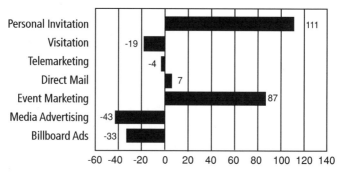

While personal invitation, event marketing (e.g., a concert or seminar), and direct mail hold value for attracting people to church, visitation, telemarketing, media advertising, and billboard ads do not. In fact, they have a negative impact on the unchurched.

Lee Strobel, a former atheist who is now a Christian, reminds his new brothers and sisters in the faith that what the unchurched need is someone to strategically venture into their environment and build a relational bridge through which the gospel can be communicated.[23]

This step is more than a rethinking—it is revolutionary. In recent years, the Christian community has developed an attitude toward the nonbelieving community that is diametrically opposed to genuine compassion for lost people. Rather than rub shoulders with irreligious people, the goal has seemed to be relational separation. Animosity toward those outside the Christian faith has often replaced genuine care and concern. As a result, most Christians have completely isolated themselves from non-Christian, unchurched people. As Barna notes, "The church-sanctioned practice of turning inward . . . to only befriend other believers . . . nullifies the evangelistic influence."[24] Yet the Bible clearly indicates that this is exactly how evangelism is to be accomplished.[25]

Step Two: Verbal Witness

The second step needed in any evangelistic enterprise is a clear, understandable verbal witness within the confines of the relationship that has been built. By verbal witness I mean the simple sharing of the Christian faith in terms that a contemporary seeker can understand.[26]

A national study revealed that Americans seek the advice of family and friends for those issues of highest importance where trust is most desired, such as who to go to for medical help or legal advice. The greater the importance, the more we turn to those we know.[27]

Though many fear annoying their friends with spiritual conversations, research shows that there is no annoyance at all when the spiritual conversation is held with a family member, close friend, or trusted associate.[28] This supports Michael Green's observation as to why the early church was so successful evangelistically: The gospel was shared like gossip over the backyard fence.[29] Sadly, only one-half of all adults who have a grace-based relationship with Christ actually share their faith in Christ with a nonbeliever during the course of a typical year.[30]

Step Three: Invitation to an Evangelistic Environment

Third, Christians must expose seekers to an environment or event that is sensitive to their spiritual situation but also clear in its presentation of the Christian faith. The goal is to offer an experience that will serve the efforts being made through the relationship being built between a Christian and a non-Christian.

Billy Graham serves as a model of this approach. His crusades are designed to interpret the Christian faith to the modern world. Graham biographer William Martin has noted that Graham's approach is to use "whatever techniques to hook 'em in, then punch 'em with the gospel. Whatever it takes to get their attention."[31] Discussing Billy Graham's 1996 Charlotte crusade decision to use such musical acts as the Charlie Daniels Band (a country group) along with rap act DC Talk, Billy Graham crusade director Rick Marshall said, "Same message with different illustrations. This is not your father's or your grandfather's Billy Graham crusade."[32] As G. A. Pritchard has noted, even earlier models can be found in "Wesley's open-air meetings, Paul's discussions in the Ephesus lecture hall, or Jesus' hillside parables."[33] The strategic importance of a Graham crusade, however, is that it is a partnership with Christians. The design is for Christians to bring their non-Christian friends to the crusade event. The hope is that the crusade, which has been uniquely designed for lost people, will team up with the relational efforts of the believers, resulting in the conversion of their non-Christian friends.

A popular way of achieving this in the local church is through what has become known as a "seeker service," which increasing numbers of churches now claim to hold.[34] This is simply a service in which a context is created that allows seekers to explore Christianity in a way that moves them "down the line" toward the event of salvation. It is a tool placed in the hands of believers to support the effort they are making with their friends. It is Billy Graham brought into the local church.

Seeker services differ in degree and style, but common dynamics within the services include anonymity, time to decide, "user-friendly" messages, the encouragement of spiritual questions, and casual dress. In essence, a safe place is created for seekers to hear and explore a very unsafe message. Such services should not be confused with worship services, for worship is usually offered as a separate service. Seeker services are services designed exclusively for seekers.[35]

Can a church do both at the same time? Conceivably, but it is highly difficult to pursue evangelism and edification—optimally—in a single service. Also, a church runs the risk of ending up in "no-man's land." This is when a church is too seeker targeted to connect with believers but not enough to reach seekers. The church ends up connecting with no one. Increasingly, the needs and questions of believers and seekers are converging, but there is a pressing need to create specific entry points that cater to those who come from an unchurched background.

Seeker services are not, however, the only way for a church to offer an evangelistic environment that will serve the relationships and verbal witnesses of individuals. Evangelistic environments are limited only to our creativity and can include small groups, special events, concerts, seminars, breakfasts, and luncheons. Being seeker targeted is the value;

a seeker service is simply a method. The goal is to assist the efforts of frontline relationships being built between Christians and non-Christians. As Bill Hybels and Mark Mittelberg have observed, "It's amazing to see how even one well-designed service, concert or program can be used by God to replace mistaken notions about Him and to open seekers to hearing more."[36]

Opening the Front Door

Keeping abreast of the importance of environment is critical, because the heart of the issue is creating an open front door, and what it takes to have an open front door changes with the culture. For example, the churches that grew the most in the 1980s and early 1990s, such as Saddleback Valley Community Church in California, Willow Creek Community Church in Chicago, Second Baptist of Houston, and even Mecklenburg, by and large had an approach during that time that I'll call the "Three R's."

Three R's of the Nineties

REASON

The first R stands for *reason*. The approach to evangelism and apologetics was to give reasons for the faith, because people already wanted to believe. They just needed to hear someone tell them why they should. Fast-growing churches built a reasoning stage into their strategy. Understanding evangelism to be both process and event, they gave seekers time to reason it out, to process it, before they decided. They needed a place to seek, and these churches gave it to them.

RELEVANCE

The second R stands for *relevance*. When a church gave people messages with practical points and an outline that could be used on Monday, it struck a chord. The church needed to show that Christianity had something to offer a life, that it was alive and contemporary, life changing and applicable—particularly contemporary. In many ways, that was the bell that needed to be rung. People needed to see and feel that the music, printing, décor, and language were related to the culture of the day instead of buried in the past. They needed to see that God was not distant and irrelevant but alive and real and ready to be engaged by contemporary persons living in the modern world.

REAL

The third R stands for *real*. One of the reasons people were turned off to church in the 1980s was because of hypocrisy, not to mention the televangelist scandals. They connected with churches that weren't phony or fake but were authentic and genuine. When leaders were willing to open up and be real about their own struggles instead of acting like they always had it together, people resonated and tended to bond.

Three E's of the Twenty-first Century

As we enter the twenty-first century, a new layer of needs has emerged that churches that grew in the 1980s and 1990s are seizing with equal vigor in light of the postmodern challenge—not in replacement of the three "R's," but in addition to them. Let's talk about them in terms of the three "E's."

EXPLANATION

The first E stands for *explanation*. Whereas the reasoned approach sought to get people to think, today we need to help people understand. It is not enough to make a case for the resurrection; the deeper need is to answer the "So what?" question. It's not "Did Jesus rise from the dead?" but "So what if he did?" It's not enough to move from the King James Version of the Bible to the New International Version or even to Eugene Peterson's *The Message* in our speaking. We have to be able to go further back and say, "This is a Bible. It has sixty-six books. There's an Old Testament and a New Testament. It tells the story of us and God." In the 1980s and early to mid 1990s, people only needed the facts, relevance, and reality of the Christian message. Today there is an increasing need to be introduced to it again for the first time. We have to talk people *to* a truth base, or truth source, instead of talking *from* one—because they're not there yet. Which is exactly what Paul did on Mars Hill. Instead of explaining how Jesus fit into a fairly developed, monotheistic worldview, such as when speaking to the God-fearing Jews in Jerusalem, Paul had to begin with very little in shared worldview—just a spiritual marketplace of ideas and a shrine to an unknown God. So he had to go back to Genesis and begin with the very identity of God.

EXPERIENCE

The second E stands for *experience*. Whereas the strategy of relevance in the 1980s helped people *apply* the faith, today people are looking for—and needing—an experience of the faith. This fleshes itself out in two ways: first, in terms of community. Today people want to belong before they believe. This is a massive shift, because most churches tend to be structured to offer belonging after believing—not simply in terms of membership, where this would need to be held up regardless, but in terms of involvement, where much more could often be done to welcome seekers into the life of the church. They are hungry for community even though they are incredibly dysfunctional in regard to community. Second, they want experience in terms of the sacred—in terms of acts and services and events that make them feel like they've done something spiritual. They want to encounter the transcendent, to experience the divine.

Back in the early nineties, seeker-targeted churches tended to have a very low participation component in the weekend services. At Mecklenburg, we would do one short chorus, get into it and out of it as quickly as possible, and then spend the rest of the service apologizing for it. I'm caricaturing that a bit, of course, but the point is that participation was to be kept to a minimum. Now we are pursuing a far more experiential element—including a sustained time of worship—on our weekends than ever before, because people are on a search for the spiritual, and what they are looking for is far more experiential than it is intellectual. Though this is an oversimplification, in the 1980s and early 1990s, people tended to believe their way into feeling. Today they tend to feel their way into believing. So things like worship, prayer, and spiritually profound or reflective moments—even the classic disciplines of the faith, such as fasting, journaling, and meditation—are more appealing to seekers than ever before. Indeed, it is what they come seeking to find.

Now the temptation would be to think that this is a throwback to traditionalism, or that perhaps the call is to return to a full-blown worship service in order to reach seekers, coming full-circle from the early boom of seeker-targeted approaches that began in the late 1970s. As I have hopefully argued here, and will argue in a different way in the chapter on worship, I do not believe this is the verdict. You can still alienate someone who is distant from the Christian faith and the life of the church with a service that is not sensitive to where that person is beginning his or her journey. What is more accurate is that there is a new, albeit thin, line that needs to be walked so that you give them just enough but not too much. But this tension has always been with the church, going back to the apostle Paul's admonishment to the Corinthian church in relation to those who might come and not understand. But make no mistake: Today there is a cry for depth, for experience, for the profound, for the sacred. People need to feel like they are getting something experientially that they can't already get in the world. So it would be the greatest of ironies if they came to church wanting to touch the transcendent and got only the world—and had to leave the church to find a sense of the holy.

EXAMPLE

The third E stands for *example*. We live in a visually oriented day, in which pictures mean everything. But to offer a visual example runs deeper than merely going visual in your services with PowerPoint and video clips (though that helps). What's more at hand is how at no time in recent memory have models and mentors meant more to those exploring the Christian faith. The effective churches of the 1980s worked hard in terms of appearing authentic. Today we need to go beyond that and present actual examples of a transformed life. The skepticism of our day is less intellectual than it is relational. Nonbelievers are skeptical of Christians as persons and as a community. It's a strange mix—people in the modern world don't believe in absolute truth, but they do believe in personal truth—so they are looking for spirituality that is genuine in terms of people's lives. It is an old line but one that rings anew: We need to *be* good news before we can *tell* good news.

A Change in Values

The key to rethinking evangelism is to understand how the world has changed, why certain approaches have worked in the past, and why they may not work in the present. But that is not all there is to rethinking evangelism; it must also involve a rethinking of values. Values are those things that we deem important and that provide direction and guidance in spite of our emotions.

I was leading a conference in Florida in which I touched on the issue of contemporary music in churches as a means to become more sensitive to those exploring the Christian faith. An elderly woman approached me afterward. It took her some time to reach me at the front of the auditorium because she walked with a cane. When she got to where I was, she said, "Young man, I want to have a word with you about what you said tonight."

I thought to myself, *Oh no, here it comes.*

She said, "Are you trying to tell me churches should use contemporary music to reach people today?"

I had just spent forty-five minutes saying just that, but I saw her cane in optimum "swing" distance, chickened out, and said, "Well, ma'am, I don't know, it might help—what do you think?"

She said, "Young man, I want you to know that about as contemporary as I get is Montovani—unless it's a weekend, and then maybe Lawrence Welk!" (You date yourself if you understand her cultural references.) Then she took her cane, held it up, and pointed it right at my face as she said, "So if rock 'n' roll is what it takes to get people back to church, all I've got to say is . . . 'Let's boogie!'"

I couldn't believe it! But then she said something I'll never forget. She said, "It's not my style of music, but if it will reach people for my Jesus, I like it. Besides," she added, "the church doesn't exist for my needs. It exists to win the world." Now *that* is rethinking the church.

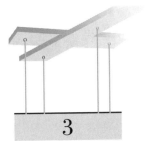

Rethinking Discipleship

John Ortberg tells of a man named Hank in a church he once pastored who had been a Christian for more than fifty years. Hank was not a happy man. He had attended church his whole life, but he had never been happy, not just about church, but about life in general. By the time John arrived, Hank was a cranky old man. He had been a member of the church since he was a cranky young man. Even the expression on his face was perpetually negative, so much so that one day a deacon asked him, "Hank, are you happy?"

Hank answered, "Yeah."

The deacon deadpanned, "Then tell your face."

Hank complained about his family and about his job. Then he was given a new object of disdain. John attempted to introduce some contemporary music into the church's services—nothing radical or outlandish, just a small step toward the twentieth century. Hank did not like contemporary music. He began to voice his concerns by saying that the music was too loud. John tried to explain to him that they were surrounded by people who did not know God and who had never met Christ, yet year after year these people drove by the church. John went on to say that, even worse, many of the people in the church weren't surprised that people kept driving by. They were not even bothered by it. John explained that as Christians they were called to enter into the world of these people, both their cultural world and their intellectual world, and to remove every barrier between them and God except the scandal of the cross. "And that," John finished, "is why we're doing what we're doing."

Hank looked at him and said, "The music is too loud."

Hank then began talking to other staff members, the ushers, even strangers in the narthex, saying, "Don't you think the music is too loud?" The leaders of the church addressed the issue and told him he had to stop. They thought it was settled until a few weeks later when a man came to the church's office, flashed his badge, and announced that he was an agent from OSHA, the Occupational Safety and Health Administration, which oversees health and safety issues in the workplace. John wondered, *Why is someone from OSHA here to see me?* The agent began explaining about dangerous decibel levels at airports and rock concerts. Then the agent told him that someone had filed a complaint about the decibel levels at the church's services, and he was under orders to investigate. Who filed the complaint? You guessed it. It was Hank. He couldn't get satisfaction anywhere else, so he called OSHA to report his church. John and the rest of his staff could only laugh. The agent joined them, saying, "Can you imagine the abuse I've been getting, coming out to bust a church?"

John's observation on the entire affair is telling: "Hank is not changing. He is a cranky guy. He has been cranky his whole life, and not just about the church. He does not effectively know how to love his wife, his children cannot relate to him, and he has no joy. He's been going to church his whole life—sixty years. And nobody is surprised! Nobody in the church is surprised that he stays cranky year after year. No one is particularly bothered by it. It is as if we expect it—that's just Hank. Nobody is expecting him to be more like Jesus year after year."[1]

Yet the Bible does expect it. The writer of Hebrews offers the following challenge:

> You have been Christians a long time now, and you ought to be teaching others. Instead, you need someone to teach you again the basic things a beginner must learn about the Scriptures. You are like babies who drink only milk and cannot eat solid food. And a person who is living on milk isn't very far along in the Christian life and doesn't know much about doing what is right.
>
> Hebrews 5:12–13 NLT

The Greek term used in the New Testament for *disciple* is *mathetes*, which simply means "learner." As Bill Hull has written, the wrong question for the church is How many people are present? The right question is What are these people like?[2] After people become Christians, the goal is for them not only to *learn* how to live like Christ, but to actually *live* like Christ. This involves nothing less than radical life change. If this is not happening, then discipleship is not happening, and rethinking must take place.

New Math, Old Math

A church can begin to rethink discipleship by thinking in terms of a mathematical equation. When it comes to life change, Christians have a tendency—knowingly or not—to write out the formula like this:

$$\text{Salvation} + \text{Time} + \text{Will} + \text{Individual Application} = \text{Life Change}$$

This formula has been developed on the basis of four basic presumptions: (1) life change happens at salvation, (2) it continues to occur naturally over time, (3) it is achieved largely by an act of the will, and (4) it is accomplished alone.

Life Change Happens at Salvation

Comedian Yakov Smirnoff says that when he first came to the United States from Russia, he wasn't prepared for the incredible variety of instant products available in American grocery stores. He says, "On my first shopping trip, I saw powdered milk—you just add water, and you get milk. Then I saw powdered orange juice—you just add water, and you get orange juice. And then I saw baby powder, and I thought to myself, *What a country!*"

Four Assumptions Commonly Made about Life Change

1. It happens at salvation.
2. It continues naturally over time.
3. It is achieved largely by an act of the will.
4. It is best accomplished alone.

One of the most basic assumptions made about life change is that it happens instantly at salvation. According to this belief, when someone gives his or her life to Christ, there is an immediate, substantive, in-depth, miraculous change in habits, attitudes, and character. As a result, disciples are born not made. The model is the "Saul to Paul" experience on the Damascus Road. Since salvation alters a person's eternal destiny and introduces the power and work of the Holy Spirit into his or her life, immediate and substantive change is not only expected but assumed.[3]

Life Change Continues Naturally over Time

While many Christians believe that most of the transformation process takes place at conversion, it is readily acknowledged that perfection is not attained when someone makes a commitment to Christ. It is often held, however, that remaining pockets of resistance are cared for through the passage of *time*. The idea is that *being* a Christian will automatically translate into *becoming* Christlike. Therefore, a five-year-old Christian will have five years' worth of spiritual maturity, a

68

ten-year-old Christian will have ten years' worth of spiritual maturity, and so on. The assumption is that faith automatically grows with time, so it is time alone that is required. As a result, many church members say, "If we can just fill the seats, then people will become disciples. All we need to do is get people to begin attending services, and they will be transformed over time into the likeness of Christ."

Life Change Is Achieved Largely by an Act of the Will

The third part of the equation involves the will. The idea is that what doesn't happen naturally over time takes place by trying. People simply need to decide to live a certain way, because living the Christian life is essentially an act of the will. Love, joy, peace, patience, kindness, goodness, faithfulness, gentleness, and self-control come when someone expends the necessary effort to demonstrate these qualities. As a result, discipleship has to do with challenging people to rise to the occasion of living the way Christ lived, because the only barrier is their level of effort.

Life Change Is Best Accomplished Alone

The final part of most discipleship equations is independence. A personal relationship with Christ has become synonymous with a private relationship with Christ. Books, seminars, classes, messages, videos, websites, and DVDs are increasingly designed for personal, private life application—and under the assumption that this is all that is needed.

Rethinking Discipleship

The question for rethinking discipleship is this: Are these assumptions valid? If they are, then working this formula in the life of the church should consistently give the same result:

a new community of people who are becoming increasingly like Jesus in their life and thought. The math should add up to increasing levels of Christlikeness. If that is not the answer a church gets when it works the equation, then it needs to rethink whether the formula is sound.

Unfortunately, many churches are not getting the correct answer.[4] In fact, a Search Institute study has found that only 11 percent of churchgoing teenagers have a well-developed faith, rising to only 32 percent for churchgoing adults.[5] Why? Because true life change only begins at salvation, takes more than just time, is about training not trying, and is a team event.

Life Change Begins at Salvation

Under the guise of correspondence between two demons concerning their "patient" on earth, C. S. Lewis explored the intricacies of spiritual growth in his masterful work *The Screwtape Letters*. Early on in the work, the human who had been the younger demon's subject of temptation becomes a Christian. The elder demon, named Screwtape, counsels his young nephew, Wormwood, not to despair, saying, "All the *habits* of the patient, both mental and bodily, are still in our favour."[6]

The Truth about Life Change

1. It begins at salvation.
2. It takes more than just time.
3. It is about training not trying.
4. It is a team event.

The insight of Lewis's Screwtape is profound. Deep, lasting life change does not often happen at salvation. The Holy Spirit can do whatever he wishes, but even the most casual observer would quickly note that he hasn't desired to do this with frequency.

When we give our life to Christ, our eternal destiny is altered, our priorities are radically reoriented, our life purpose is changed, and the Holy Spirit works in and through us by his power. Yet rather than instant liberation from every bad habit or character flaw we have ever possessed, what takes place is more like the landing of an army on a beach and the routing out of the enemy as the army makes its way inland. The event of salvation is best seen as the beginning of the pilgrimage toward life change. Even the celebrated case of Paul's conversion is simply that—the story of his conversion. It is widely believed that what followed was a lengthy time of mentoring and discipleship.[7] Just as there is a process that leads up to the event of salvation, so there is a process that begins after the event of salvation and moves us toward life change. Eugene Peterson rightly called the process of discipleship "a long obedience in the same direction."[8]

Life Change Takes More Than Just Time

I first picked up the game of golf when I was in graduate school. I took some lessons from a course pro, bought a set of clubs, and began to play fairly regularly. Initially, I made excellent progress, but then I began to play with less and less frequency. Soon I played only at the annual Christmas gathering with my wife's family. And as you might expect, I would play at about the same level each year because I hadn't played since the previous year.

Recently, I started to play with more regularity, and my game has improved dramatically. If someone asks me how long I've played, however, my answer would not be a fair indicator of my level of skill. I could tell them I've played for more than two decades. The problem is I haven't been intentional about the game during that entire time. People who have been playing the game only a year but have been committed to it could easily outplay me.

It is no different with our spiritual life. Simply being exposed to information does not mean that people absorb it, understand it, or embrace it. For example, George Barna has discovered that among born-again Christians, 80 percent could not define the Great Commission as the marching orders of Jesus for the church. Only half know that John 3:16 is a verse that addresses salvation.[9] The challenge is even greater for issues related to lifestyle.

While discipleship takes time, it is not merely a product of time or a by-product of mere "exposure" to the Christian subculture. Churches are full of individuals who have spent years as Christians yet live lives that reflect little of the fruit of the Holy Spirit. The reason for this is simple: Life change is not a question of time as much as intentionality. The writer of Hebrews understood this, writing that "though by this time you ought to be teachers, you need someone to teach you the elementary truths of God's word all over again" (Heb. 5:12).

Life Change Is about Training, Not Trying

Merely trying to experience life change can never bring about life change. I can try very hard to bench-press three hundred pounds, but that isn't what will enable me to do it. I will only be able to bench-press three hundred pounds by training to bench-press three hundred pounds.

Michael Jordan is arguably the greatest basketball player ever to have played in the history of the National Basketball Association. A whole generation of basketball players has grown up wanting to be "just like Mike." They wanted to shoot like Mike, jump like Mike, jam like Mike, and most importantly, have their tongue hang out like Mike's.

To assume that someone becomes a disciple of Christ simply by trying would be similar to saying that all someone has to do to play like Jordan is to try to play like Jordan. But here's what happens. When a person is playing in a basketball game, he tries to act just like Jordan acts—to jump, shoot, dribble, and pass just like he does. This person holds his head like Jordan does, positions his arms the way he does, buys his shoes and then ties them the way he does, wears an armband where he does, and then this person expects to play like he does. But he doesn't, and the reason he fails is because he is trying to play the way Jordan plays in a game.

But that is not how Jordan plays the game. He achieved his endless winning performances not by behaving a certain way during a game but through an overall life of preparation and practice. The jumps, acrobatics, timing, and ability didn't come through his game time but through his practice time. The two or three hours of breathtaking performance came because of his countless hours of practice and training and eating the right diet.[10]

To play like Michael Jordan, we don't try; we train. We do the things he does in order to perform at game time like he does. And to live like Jesus, we don't try either. We train. We do the things Jesus did in order to live like Jesus lived. That's why Jesus said, "Everyone who is *fully trained* will be like his teacher" (Luke 6:40, italics added). And the apostle Paul wrote, "*Train yourself* to be godly" (1 Tim. 4:7, italics added; see also 1 Cor. 9:24–26). The key to life change, to truly living a Christlike life, is to order our life around those activities, disciplines, and practices that were modeled by Christ, in order to accomplish through training what we cannot now do by trying.[11]

Life Change Is a Team Event

If you have ever experienced or are familiar with Alcoholics Anonymous, you know that this group has an astounding record for authentic life change. Lives devastated and controlled by the abuse of alcohol discover radical transformation through AA's program. What is the secret? Many would say it is due to the buddy system. If a member feels the urge to drink, that person is supposed to call someone who will support his or her effort not to do it. People do call, and as a result, they receive support for their life change. But it goes deeper than that. Every aspect of Alcoholics Anonymous is saturated with the relational element. Participants meet weekly as a group for sharing and support; plus they have small group meetings and a one-on-one buddy system. AA capitalizes on the importance of a relational component to true transformation.

Until recent times, almost every form of education was relational in nature, usually in the form of mentoring. For example, in colonial America, one would serve as an apprentice for six years to a particular tradesperson in order to learn a craft. The apprentice would live, eat, and breathe with the person he wanted to emulate in terms of a skill.

This insight is taught throughout the Bible. In Proverbs, we read, "As iron sharpens iron, so one man sharpens another" (27: 17). The writer of Hebrews said, "Let us consider how we may spur one another on toward love and good deeds. Let us not give up meeting together, as some are in the habit of doing, but let us encourage one another" (10:24–25). Throughout the Bible, in the lives of those who developed their faith in God, there is a dedication to key relationships. Jethro mentored his son-in-law Moses. Moses then turned around and made a relational contribution to the life of his successor, Joshua. The prophet Elijah poured his life into the prophet Elisha. Mary, the mother of Jesus, turned to her older cousin, Elizabeth, for help. And Jesus set apart twelve men in order to invest his life in theirs.

Optimal growth occurs when we develop a relationship with someone who knows something we don't or has experience in an area we don't and is willing to share this knowledge with us. The heart of Christian development has long been a relationship between someone who has something to learn and someone who has something to share. In the context of such a relationship, a synergy develops that accelerates and enhances growth. Synergy is the energy or force that is generated through the working together of various parts or processes. For example, two horses can pull about nine thousand pounds, but through the power created by adding more horses, four horses can pull more than thirty thousand pounds. This is the essence of synergy. In his classic economics text, *The Wealth of Nations,* Adam Smith wrote that ten people working individually can produce twenty pins a day, but ten people working together can produce forty-eight thousand pins a day. The point is simple: When we start developing key relationships in our lives or add people to help us in life, the impact is phenomenal. A married couple will tell us of the benefit of a Christian counselor. An athlete will talk about the importance of a trainer or a coach. A businessperson will talk about the power of a team. In life, we all need support—and when we get it, it makes all the difference in the world. Discipleship was never intended to be a solo event. Such things as accountability, ongoing challenge, encouragement, and personal support are impossible apart from other people.

Discipleship That Disciples

Effective discipleship involves writing the equation a new way:

Salvation + Intentionality + Training + Community = Life Change

Rethinking discipleship, however, involves more than simply creating a new set of assumptions. Rethinking the equation is one thing; rethinking the existing process of discipleship, which has been based on the equation, is something else altogether. It is the development of a new process that is at the heart of rethinking. The goal is to take the new equation, with its radically different set of assumptions, and redesign the discipleship process in such a way as to actually enable individuals to become increasingly like Christ. Again, the key word is process, because the rethinking must involve a complete end-to-end set of activities that together provide the necessary training and relationships for true spiritual growth. The heart of rethinking discipleship in the church is this: understanding the dynamics of life change in such a way as to develop a biblical process that equips and empowers people to become increasingly like

Christ. Though the process itself can be developed in countless ways, two components are vital.

Training on Training

The first component that a church must provide is training on training. People must be coached as to the training regimen needed to become increasingly like Christ. Most books, classes, sermons, seminars, tapes, and videos attempt to pass on information or issue challenges, yet few are specifically designed to actually equip people for the training regimen they will need to follow in order to become more like Christ. For example, does your church offer training on how to have a daily quiet time? Notice that I didn't ask if members have been *taught* to have one or *challenged* to have one, but if they have been *trained* as to how to have one. Effective discipleship will help people learn how to order their life around the attitudes, practices, disciplines, relationships, and experiences of Christ. Once trained in this way, they are able to enter into training for themselves—training that will allow them to become increasingly like Christ.

At Mecklenburg, we have developed an overarching strategy for the entire mission of the church built around the words "Team," "Train," and "Game." First, people need to join the team. Under this is our entire outreach and assimilation strategy. Then, under "Train," is our effort toward discipleship. Finally comes "Game," which is about contributing to the mission as a participating player. Using "Train" as an acrostic, we have outlined five principal areas for spiritual development:

Teaching
Relationships
Attributes
Investments
Needs

T stands for the *teaching*, or knowledge, component in the life of a disciple. A Christ-follower should know certain things about God, the Bible, Jesus, the Holy Spirit, humanity, the end times, the Christian life, and the church.

R stands for *relationships*. One of the key ideas within discipleship is that life change happens best in the context of relationships. So we work hard at helping people into key relationships, particularly through our network of small groups (see below).

A stands for *attributes*. One of the key dynamics of discipleship is that we become more like Jesus every year. A very important focus of spiritual formation has to do with becoming more loving, truthful, patient, kind, generous, peaceful, gentle, and yielded to the work of the Holy Spirit in our lives.

I stands for *investments*. Certain spiritual practices and disciplines are essential to spiritual growth, including quiet times, prayer, Bible study, journaling, retreats, silence, solitude, fasting, and stewardship.

N stands for *needs*—specifically the needs of others. A disciple is someone who has a heart for the needs present in the lives of others and wants to meet those needs. This means a heart for serving, a heart for ministry, a heart for the poor and destitute.

While we have developed a number of classes and experiences, sermon series and seminars to support all five areas, we have also fashioned a "gateway" experience that introduces individuals to the life of training called "Training Camp," coupled with a personal assessment tool that helps people identify where they are with each area and what the best next steps are for them to take. The goal of such efforts is simple: Rather than simply telling people to "dunk the ball," churches must take them into the gym and show them how to train and practice for the game itself.[12]

Opportunities for Relationships

A second crucial component of the discipleship process is strategic opportunities for relationships. Life change happens best through relationships, and while large group events are well suited for certain aspects of Christian growth, Lynne and Bill Hybels are correct in noting that "there appears to be a Holy Spirit–prompted migration in which Christians gravitate toward smaller gatherings so they can experience the life change that occurs most optimally in community."[13] Through community in smaller settings, we receive four critical infusions: We get strength for life's storms; we receive wisdom for making important decisions; we experience accountability, which is vital to spiritual growth; and we find acceptance that helps us repair our wounds.[14]

As a result, various types of small groups—and particularly the mentoring relationships they generate—"provide the optimal environment for incubating the maturing process. Where there is trust and transparency, and where there are extended periods of time to help each other apply biblical truth to real-life situations, suddenly scriptural truths that seemed theoretical become concrete and practical."[15] Small groups are just that—small groups of people that get together to build relationships, study the Bible, and encourage each other in the faith.[16] They are small communities within the larger community in which people can experience the forgiveness, healing, and growth they need. They are Christian friends who become a support group for believers and their faith. As the writer of Ecclesiastes says, "Two are better than one, because they have a good return for their work: If one falls down, his friend can help him up. But pity the man who falls and has no one to help him up!" (4:9–10). Therefore, the question that must be asked is this: What type of small group network provides the optimal setting for transformational community to take place within a church?

There is no doubt that small groups can successfully take many forms, including the traditional age-graded Sunday school. As my friend Thom Rainer has written, "Contrary to the views of some of its critics, effective Sunday Schools are not archaic in their methodology. No traditional organization can survive for two centuries without methodological adaptation."[17] Yet many churches that use a Sunday school program do not seem to benefit from the life-changing power of community, much less find it serving their church as an effective mechanism for discipleship.[18] So the question isn't as simple as developing just any small group system. A network of small groups must be developed that produces the relationships needed for discipleship to take place.[19] Regardless of the process developed, nothing could be deadlier than for a church to say, "Well, we know Sunday school and understand Sunday school, so whether or not it's best, we'll just keep doing it that way because it would be too much trouble to change."[20] At Mecklenburg, our small groups are known as Home Teams, and they meet at different times and places throughout the community and reflect any number of forms—from couples' groups to men's groups, recovery and support groups to seeker groups.[21]

No Quick Fix

One summer my family and I vacationed at Emerald Isle, North Carolina. Near Emerald Isle is a little city called Beaufort. It is one of the oldest towns in North Carolina and is rich in history. Visitors can take a tour of several buildings that date back as far as 1706. One of the buildings is an apothecary. When we went through it, we saw all kinds of wonder drugs guaranteed to cure anything that were sold between one hundred and two hundred years ago. The ingredients listed on the side of a bottle of "Oil of Youth" were 2 percent ether, 4 percent chloroform, and 60 percent alcohol. It said it could be taken internally or applied externally, and it promised to cure asthma, fever, coughing, colds, diarrhea, kidney trouble, and nerves. And at 60 percent alcohol, I'll bet it did help one's nerves! "Dr. DeWitt's Eclectic Remedy" could be used for cramps. A bottle labeled "Blood Syrup" promised it would heal the liver, clean the blood, tone one's stomach, open one's pores, and regulate one's bowels. There was no lack of sales, because people wanted a quick fix. Unfortunately, most of these remedies did not do all the things they claimed to do.

Life change cannot be achieved through a quick fix either. It is not a onetime event; it is a process that must be developed in light of how people actually are transformed into the likeness of Christ. And that takes some rethinking.

4

Rethinking Ministry

Bill Hybels, in his book *Honest to God,* describes the ritual that often takes place in churches when it comes to the practice of ministry. The pastor—we'll call him Bob—has just received his annual flood of resignations from Sunday school teachers, nursery workers, ushers, and youth workers, all of whom want out. Pastor Bob isn't really surprised—it happens every year. Some offer lengthy explanations; some just say they've done their part.

Pastor Bob knows that the ministries of the church cannot continue unless somebody fills these positions, so he gears up for his annual recruitment campaign. But not only is Pastor Bob gearing up for the annual affair, so are the members of his church. They know Pastor Bob is going to be coming after them to serve, and they are already thinking about how they are going to turn him down. John, a deacon, says to himself, *He's not going to get me this year. So help me, I don't care what he preaches on or how often he threatens God's judgment. I'm not going to cave in—even if he starts to cry! Three years ago he cried, and I ended up as a center aisle usher—and I don't even like people! This year I'll resist to the end.*

Pastor Bob knows he will encounter serious resistance, so this year he is bringing out the heavy artillery. He's planning a four-part series called "Serve or Burn." Every sermon will begin with an illustration from Foxe's *Book of Martyrs*. He has already decided to wear a lapel microphone so he can walk the length of the stage. He will raise his voice, perspire a little bit, and wave his Bible in the air. On the fourth week, he will bring out his secret weapon—seven-year-old Suzi Miller. He will cradle the little darling on his lap and ask her what it will be like to spend a whole year in her second grade Sunday school class without a teacher. He hopes against hope that she will cry. If she does, he will win the war hands down.

Pastor Bob's strategy works. The "Serve or Burn" series goes better than he expected. Little Suzi cries on cue. People feel worn down and guilty. By September 1, the empty positions are filled for another year.[1]

The Traditional Approach to Ministry

Pastor Bob's approach to ministry is all too common. Essentially, it is a five-step process.

1. Begin with a Program

According to the traditional approach to ministry, a church begins with a program. A vast majority of churches have a program-based design, which means that their ministries are based on programs that have been imported from outside the church. Many denominations have as their central responsibility the development of programs for churches to employ. Some of the programs meet a need, but many are employed by churches out of denominational loyalty or even denominational pressure. Just as common is employing a program due to another church's success, hoping for a silver bullet through a one-size-fits-all approach. In fact, programs

82

from famed megachurches have often become akin to a new denominational supply line.

2. Find Some People

After the leaders of a church have decided on a program, the next step is to find the people who will run the program. Several positions need to be filled. In most cases, those doing the recruiting only provide a potential volunteer with the name of the position and possibly a job description. All the volunteers need to bring to the table is a pulse.

3. Sell the Program

After the program is staffed, it is then promoted in the church. Sometimes the promotion is tied in with what the program will do for people, but more often than not the members of the church are asked to support the program for the program's sake. It may or may not meet a need, but once in place, the program itself becomes the need, and people are challenged to get behind the program in order to see results. This is particularly true for denominational programs, as they are often couched in terms of a mission initiative.

The Traditional Approach to Ministry

1. Begin with a program.
2. Find some people.
3. Sell the program.
4. Carry out the program.
5. Maintain the program.

4. Carry Out the Program

The next step is to carry out the program. In the movie *Field of Dreams,* Kevin Costner's character hears a voice that says, "If you build it, they will come." The voice is telling him that if he builds a baseball field, people will automatically come to the field. All he has to do is build the field. The same idea is behind this fourth step in the traditional approach to ministry. If church members *do* the program, the program will *do* the ministry. Whether the ministry involves trying to meet a specific shepherding need, generating an increase in attendance, stimulating financial giving, or creating an interest in world missions, the church members stand back with both expectation and a sense of accomplishment. They *did* stewardship, or missions, or evangelism because they did the *program*—when in reality the program may not have accomplished any of the objectives of the ministry.

5. Maintain the Program

The final step in the approach to ministry employed by many churches is to maintain the program—no matter what. It is almost an unwritten rule that once a program begins, it cannot be allowed to end. That would be a ministry failure, or even worse, denominational or missional disloyalty. If the program does not work as promised, the problem is considered to be with the church not the program. As a result, the church often responds by investing more people, more money, and more promotion into the program. Even if the failure is so acute that the ministry has become nothing more than an inactive oversight committee, the committee is often maintained—even if only on paper—because eliminating the program would be seen as eliminating the church's efforts in that area. As long as a program is there, the feeling that ministry is taking place is there.

Rethinking Ministry

Webster's New World Dictionary defines *ministry* as "that which serves." A ministry, therefore, is that which actually meets a need. For a need to be met, two things have to be in place: (1) a real need and (2) a person or resource that can effectively meet that need. Obvious? Of course. But it's amazing how the obvious can become obscured over time.

Real Needs

I once read about a young Boy Scout who was asked by his scoutmaster if he had done his good deed for the day. The young boy said he didn't think he had. The scoutmaster told the boy to go out and do his good deed for the day and not return until he had.

The little boy left, but he came back in less than twenty minutes. His clothes were in shreds, his hair was sticking out, and his face was cut and bleeding.

The scoutmaster said, "Goodness, boy, what have you been doing?"

The boy said, "I did my good deed for the day, sir."

"What did you do?" the scoutmaster asked.

"I helped an old lady cross the street," said the young scout.

Confused, the scoutmaster said, "Then how did you get in this condition? Your clothes are torn, your hair is messed up, your face is cut and bleeding . . . what happened?"

The boy said, "Well, she didn't exactly want to go."

The goal of ministry is to meet a need that exists in the lives of people. If a ministry does not meet a need, then it is not a ministry. A wonderful program may exist for a particular activity and be meeting a pressing need in another context, but for the program to be a ministry in *your* church, it must meet a need in *your* church or community.

In the movie *Big*, Tom Hanks plays a twelve-year-old boy who, overnight, physically becomes a man yet remains a young boy on the inside. One day, as he is playing in an FAO Schwarz toy store, the president of the toy company recognizes him for what he is: the perfect toy company employee. Hanks is hired and soon demonstrates that he knows what will appeal to children because he is a child himself. Others guess at the needs and wants of kids—Hanks's character *knows*. When the president gives him the ability to make product decisions, he provides the toy company with an overwhelming competitive advantage.

The most effective ministries in churches are those that are based on knowledge of the needs and interests of the people to whom a church is trying to minister. No one is better poised to make that assessment—and create the proper response—than the church itself.

Resources to Meet Existing Needs

According to a study conducted in 1991, only 27 percent of all adults devoted any amount of time to assisting their church during the prior week. When the study was repeated in 2002, the figure had dropped to 24 percent.[2] In spite of near universal affirmation of the importance of volunteering and serving others, something is not connecting. And much of it lies in relating people to ministry itself.

A school newsletter once published this story:

> Once upon a time, the animals decided they should do something meaningful to meet the problems of the new world. So they organized a school. They adopted an activity curriculum of running, climbing, swimming and flying. To make it easier to administer the curriculum, all the animals took all the subjects. The duck was excellent in swimming, in fact, better than his instructor. But he made only passing grades in flying and was very poor in running. Since he was slow in running, he had to drop swimming and stay after school to practice running. This caused his webbed feet to be badly worn so that he was only average in swimming. But average was quite acceptable, so nobody worried about that—except the duck. The rabbit started at the top of his class in running but developed a nervous twitch in his leg muscles because of so much make-up work in swimming. The squirrel was excellent in climbing, but he encountered constant frustration in flying

class because the teacher made him start from the ground up instead of from the treetop down. He developed "charlie horses" from overexertion and so only got a C in climbing and a D in running. The eagle was a problem child and was severely disciplined for being a nonconformist. In climbing classes he beat all the others to the top of the tree but insisted on using his own way to get there.[3]

The same negative results can take place in a church when people are forced into roles for which they are not suited. Remember our story about Pastor Bob? There is no joy in serving God when it is done for the wrong reasons. The people in Pastor Bob's church served out of guilt, to get the pastor off their back, or maybe just to look good to other people. And because the pastor's primary concern was filling positions, members often ended up serving in the wrong places in light of their gifts and abilities. When that happens, members are not effective in meeting the need they are attempting to meet. The church ends up with teachers who can't teach, leaders who can't lead, administrators who can't administrate, and singers who can't carry a tune. For a ministry to meet a need, the need must be met. This is why the Bible encourages us to begin by fitting people into appropriate areas of ministry and does so by teaching three important truths about gifts and ministry.

1. The Bible teaches that *every* Christian, not just the ordained clergy of the church, is a minister.[4] Paul wrote to the church at Ephesus that "[Christ] gave some to be apostles, some to be prophets, some to be evangelists, and some to be pastors and teachers, to prepare God's people for works of service, so that the body of Christ may be built up" (Eph. 4:11–12).

2. At conversion, every Christian is given at least one spiritual gift that is to be used for the purpose of ministry (see Rom. 12:3–8; 1 Cor. 12; Eph. 4:1–16). In Ephesians, Paul writes, "Christ has given each of us special abilities—whatever he wants us to have out of his rich storehouse of gifts"

(4:7 TLB). In Romans, Paul writes, "God has given each of us the ability to do certain things well" (12:6 TLB). A spiritual gift is a supernatural capacity to develop a particular ability for kingdom service. There are speaking gifts, such as teaching; people gifts, such as counseling, encouragement, evangelism, hospitality, leadership, and mercy; service gifts, such as administration, giving, and helps; and support gifts, such as faith and wisdom. No one has all the gifts. In Romans we read, "Just as each of us has one body with many members, and these members do not all have the same function, so in Christ we who are many form one body. . . . We have different gifts" (12:4–6).

The Bible and Ministry

1. Every Christian is a minister.
2. At conversion, every Christian is given at least one spiritual gift that is to be used for ministry.
3. We are to operate in the area of our gifts.

---

3. The Bible teaches that we are to operate in the area of our gifts. Christians believe that the church is supernatural in its origin, but it is easy to forget that it is also supernatural in its operation. As Paul wrote to the church at Corinth, "The Holy Spirit displays God's power through each of us as a means of helping the entire church" (1 Cor. 12:7 TLB). This is important for ministry, as noted by Bill Hybels in his reflections on Pastor Bob's approach to finding volunteers.

> Speaking of mercy, it's no secret to those who know me that I don't have that gift. Not long ago at an elders' meeting I prayed with a dear woman from our church who is slowly dying of diabetes. As much as I loved this woman and wanted to minister to her, I was painfully aware of my awkwardness. I just don't function well in situations like that. After I left this woman, another elder approached her. Without hesitation he wrapped his arms around her, kissed her on the cheek, and said, "Oh, Jane, I'm so glad you're here tonight." While he held her hand she wept. Because he was so natural and tender, she

could really feel his love and concern. I thought, "Lord, thank you for giving him that beautiful gift of mercy. Thank you for prompting him to use it here tonight."[5]

Bill knew that there were others who were more gifted at showing mercy than he was, and he was willing to let them serve where they were gifted. Churches need to rethink ministry in the same way. The result of this rethinking is not just effective ministry but an increase in volunteers. George Barna observes that one of the oddities about American participation in ministry is that people do not get involved because it is the right thing to do. More often, people get involved because they believe they can make a positive difference by utilizing their unique talents and abilities.[6]

A Ministry Development Process

From these rethinkings, the goal is to create a process by which effective ministry is created, implemented, and sustained. Though the specifics will take various forms within individual churches, the following steps are integral to the rethinking and the development of a new ministry process.

1. Start with a Need

First, a church must start with a need. A ministry should not be considered unless it meets a specific need in the life of your particular church. Just because someone is willing, or a ministry meets a need in another church, or the church is encouraged by a denomination, parachurch group, megachurch, or association to take part does not mean a need for a particular ministry exists in your church.

This means that a strategy for listening to people must be in place in order to determine the needs of a church. A question as simple as How can this church better serve you and your family's needs? can revolutionize a church. Why? Because effective ministry starts with a need, and needs are discovered through effective listening.

2. Match the Need with the Mission

The second step in a ministry process involves matching the need with the mission. There are countless needs that can be met, but not all fall under the purposes and mission of a church. In fact, an attempt to meet some needs could actually hurt a church's commitment to its purposes and mission. The story of the lighthouse keeper in chapter 1 illustrates this concern. Limited resources must be allocated strategically in order to cover the foundational purposes and mission of a church, else they will suffer. Ministry should be informed by the needs of those a church is trying to minister to, but needs alone should not drive the ministry of a church. Only when a ministry meets a need and supports the purposes and mission of the church should it be pursued.

3. Wait for a Leader

The third step in the ministry development process involves waiting for a Spirit-gifted and Spirit-called leader. When a need that matches a church's purposes and mission is discovered, the temptation is to launch out into that ministry immediately. Yet a ministry without a leader is doomed to suffer if not fail. The people involved in that ministry will also suffer. No one is served if a ministry is not well led.

4. Build according to Giftedness

Several years ago, a movie called *Chariots of Fire* captured the attention of millions of people. The movie is about Eric Liddell, an Olympic runner in the 1930s from Scotland. In the film, Jenny, Liddell's sister, questions him about why he is going to run in the Olympics instead of pursuing another career. In reply, he turns to his sister and says, "Jenny, God made me fast, and when I run, I feel his pleasure."

God made all of us a certain way, and when we serve in that way, we feel pleasure—God's and ours. The fourth step in rethinking any ministry process should grapple with this truth. A ministry team must be built according to giftedness. Rather than merely filling in slots on an organizational chart with names of people willing to serve, the process of finding people to serve in a particular ministry should involve determining what spiritual gifts are needed for a particular role and then matching people with those gifts to that role.[7] By following this approach, a church will have teachers teaching, leaders leading, administrators administrating, and counselors counseling. This is one of the goals of the third element of Mecklenburg's overarching strategy, under the heading of "Game." To get people into the game involves finding the position that God has designed for them.

Ministry Development Process

1. Start with a need.
2. Match the need with the mission.
3. Wait for a leader.
4. Build according to giftedness.
5. Review regularly.

5. Review Regularly

The final step in the process involves review. All ministries should be evaluated regularly to determine whether they continue to meet a need, continue to serve the purposes and mission of a church, continue to be well led, and continue to have the necessary team of Spirit-gifted people in place. If one or more of these goals is no longer being met, the ministry should be ended, or at the very least, temporarily suspended while the deficiency is addressed.

Important as this step is in the process, however, it is rare. Far more common is the ministry that is sustained long after the necessary components for its success are present. The ministry becomes a monument—immovable and carved in stone—and a church begins to serve the ministry rather than the ministry serving the church.

Yet the research of James C. Collins and Jerry I. Porras shows that the most effective organizations are those that made their most creative developments through trial and error.[8] They describe the process as "branching and pruning." The idea is simple: "If you add enough branches to a tree and intelligently prune the deadwood, then you'll likely evolve into a collection of healthy branches well positioned to prosper in an ever-changing environment."[9] Mistakes will be made. The question is whether those mistakes will be acknowledged. Our tendency is to be willing to branch—just not prune. Yet both are vital to any church's ongoing vitality and effectiveness.

The Need for New Colors

Henry Ford built an empire on the Model T automobile. But it wasn't the automobile itself that catapulted Ford into an empire. It was the way the car was made. Ford established a new approach to manufacturing called the moving assembly line, which he perfected in 1913. This enabled him to triple previous rates of production and make cars affordable to virtually anyone. His black Model T, the world's best-selling car for many years, could be purchased in 1924 for as little as $290. But when consumers came forward and asked for cars in different colors, Ford quipped that they could have their car in any color they wanted—as long as it was black.

Ford was able to go a long way on that approach but only due to the novelty of the Model T, his domination of the market, and the ability to undersell his few competitors through mass production. It wasn't long, of course, before "any color as long as it's black" was insufficient; people's needs just weren't being served.

Rethinking ministry means rethinking the attitude "any color as long as it's black." A ministry should meet a need. If that means a new color is called for, break out the paint.

5

Rethinking Worship

The King James Version of the Bible is a beautiful translation of the Hebrew and Greek manuscripts into the English language as it was spoken in the seventeenth century. During that time it was common for people to say "thee" and "thou," and therefore, the King James Version uses "thee" and "thou." Neither Jesus nor the apostle Paul spoke in King James English, but the people of the seventeenth century did, and that's one of the reasons why the King James Version became such a meaningful and beloved translation.

As time passed, however, the King James Version became increasingly distanced from the way in which people expressed themselves. This made the translation more difficult to understand and less meaningful to read. People simply expressed themselves differently in the nineteenth and twentieth centuries than they did in the seventeenth century. "Thee" and "thou" became "you"; "whither" became "where"; "nought" became "nothing"; and "speaketh" and "getteth" became "speaks" and "gets."

As a result of the changing nature of language, newer translations began to appear, such as the Revised Standard Version, the New International Version, and the Contemporary English Version. Yet for centuries the King James Version existed as the only accepted English translation of the Bible, long after King James English was the dominant form of verbal expression in the English-speaking world, because people confused the King James language with the original text of the Bible itself. Each effort to create a new translation, however, involved a return to the ancient Scriptures and a careful translation of the original text into a more contemporary form of expression. The result? Readers are able to read the Bible with better understanding.

The lesson learned in regard to Bible versions can also be applied to worship. The word *worship* is from the Anglo-Saxon word *weorthscipe*, which literally reads "worth-ship." Worship is the expression of honor and respect to someone or something. For Christians, it is expressing honor and love to God. This worship should not only be biblical but meaningful, for to attempt to express honor to God in a way that is not meaningful would not be worship. Worship without meaning would incur the indictment given by Jesus to the Pharisees and the teachers of the law: "These people honor me with their lips, but their hearts are far from me. They worship me in vain" (Matt. 15:8–9). Therefore, worship is that which authentically and meaningfully expresses honor, love, and devotion to God.[1] Just as attempting to read the Bible in King James English can prevent the Word of God from being understood and applied by a modern reader, worship that uses outdated cultural forms can inhibit the full expression of worship.

The Unstated Assumptions

The worshiping life of most churches is largely built on two assumptions that are seldom verbalized yet are highly influential. The first is that worship should be traditional in its expression, and second, that it is an event solely for the believer and, as a result, is irrelevant to non-Christians.

1. *Worship should be traditional.* An unstated assumption in many churches regarding worship is that for it to be worship it must be traditional. The word *traditional* is highly subjective, for what is traditional to one person may be innovative to another, but the essence of a tradition is universal: the ongoing preservation of a practice from the past. This assumption is more than a heartfelt desire to maintain rich biblical and historical practices that have clearly served Christians over the last two thousand years. Rather, it is the feeling that *only* that which is from a past era is appropriate as a vehicle for worship. As a result, many churches use the music, instruments, clothing, language, and décor of past eras.

> **Two Unstated Assumptions about Worship**
>
> 1. Worship should be traditional.
> 2. Worship is irrelevant to non-Christians.

2. *Worship is irrelevant to non-Christians.* The second belief held by many churches is that worship is an event and experience for believers, and therefore, it is irrelevant to non-Christians. The Bible clearly teaches that there is at least one act of worship—the Lord's Supper—that should not be practiced by those who are outside of a relationship with Christ. Yet the assumption that worship is irrelevant to non-Christians goes well beyond this concern. Those who hold this assumption believe that since non-Christians would have neither the desire nor the ability to truly worship God, it is not important whether they connect with the service at all. It does not matter whether they are able to appreciate the music, understand the ritual, or benefit from the message. The unstated assumption is that worship is for *us*, not for *them*.

Rethinking Worship

These two assumptions are at the heart of the worshiping life of many churches. Yet rethinking the church demands that churches ask whether these assumptions are sound ones to make, beginning with traditionalism.

Leith Anderson tells of a desperate church. Years of decline had taken a painful toll. "What we need," the members said, "is a dynamic new pastor." A search committee did everything right to find the perfect leader. He was young but experienced, serious but witty, articulate but not intimidating, spiritual but world wise. If anyone could turn this problem-ridden congregation around, he was the man.

When the pastoral candidate first addressed the congregation, he gave an inspiring description of his qualifications, experience, vision, and plans. His final line summed up his stirring presentation: "With God's help, I intend to lead this church forward into the twentieth century!" Surprised and embarrassed by the candidate's apparent mistake, the chairman of the search committee whispered loudly, "You mean 'the twenty-first century'!" to which the candidate replied, "We're going to take this one century at a time!"[2]

Church members must ask themselves, "In what century does our worship reside?" The King James Version of the Bible spoke beautifully and effectively to seventeenth-century people. While still beautiful in its prose, it has lost much of its effectiveness as a translation. The goal of recent efforts, such as the New International Version, has been to remain faithful to the original manuscripts while updating the language for today. The goal of worship must be similar: preserving the traditions that are crucial to remaining biblical and to staying connected with the past, but avoiding the practice of simply preserving a custom for its own sake. But because so many churches believe that worship must be traditional to be worship, it is traditional*ism* that is carrying the day. As church consultant Bob Logan has written, an "amazing phenomenon in the . . . church is that we are still stuck in forms of worship and ministry which are more culturally appropriate to the nineteenth century. The robes, the pipe organ, the hymnals, the order of worship, and the nature and place of the sermon are all vestiges of nineteenth-century culture."[3]

The result is a King James Version of worship in a cyberspace world, which has led to a weakened sense of worship in the life of the church. For example, the Evangelical Lutheran Church in America asked pastors and laity if theirs was a church with vibrant worship. While 57 percent of the clergy—the ones who led worship—said yes, only 28 percent of the laity agreed.[4] Larger studies indicate that seven out of ten adults (71 percent) say they have *never* experienced God's presence at a church service.[5] Of those who regularly attend, one in three concur, saying that they have never experienced God through their church's worship service.[6] This mind-set was expressed candidly by an individual attending a national denominational event who humorously wrote on an evaluation form, "I felt stoned to death by the rock of ages."[7] When a service attempts to provide an opportunity for people to express themselves in worship to God yet does so in a culturally outdated or incomprehensible form, there is a loss of meaning.

And what of the assumption that worship is irrelevant to those outside the church? In most American churches, the weekend worship service has become the "front door" of the church, meaning that it is the primary entry point for people to explore the church and, as a result, its message.[8] Prior to the early 1970s, the main point of entry was the Sunday school, but this has changed. In the Southern Baptist Convention, which continues to work as hard as anyone to promote the Sunday school as the primary entry point of the church, average worship attendance far outpaces average Sunday school attendance and has since 1971.[9] While Sunday school attendance increased between 2001 and 2002 from its multiyear plateau of around 19 percent to 25 percent, this still only constitutes one out of every four adults.[10] As pastor and author Kennon Callahan has written,

> Worship is extraordinarily important in the unchurched culture in which we are engaged in mission. That is, it is highly

likely that many of the unchurched persons whom a church reaches in mission or visitation will find their way first to the service of worship. In the 1950s and early 1960s, it was frequently the case that unchurched persons found their way into the life and mission of the local congregation through a small group. Indeed, much emphasis was placed upon this. This still occurs, but now more often unchurched persons find their way first to the service of worship. Thus, corporate, dynamic worship becomes an increasingly important avenue through which people are reached on behalf of Christ.[11]

Only a Christian can truly worship God in spirit and truth. Yet non-Christians often begin their exploration of the Christian faith through the worship services of believers. As Rick Warren has observed, nonbelievers can watch believers worship, and that worship can be a powerful witness to them if God's presence is felt and if the message is understandable.[12] Throughout the Bible there is a close, vibrant relationship between worship and evangelism, so much so that the apostle Paul chastised the Corinthian church for worshiping in a way that would make little sense to a first-time guest (1 Cor. 14: 23–25). And if the worship experience has lost its meaning for the believer, imagine its irrelevance to the nonbeliever.

Opening the Front Door

Worship is an emotionally sensitive issue simply because a preferred style of worship is often a reflection of a person's personality. We are simply far too prone to build theological walls around our personal tastes.[13] The issue for rethinking, however, has little to do with any specific style. Different churches should employ different styles of worship, not to mention a wide range of traditions, in order to fit different kinds of personalities.

Rethinking worship has more to do with the assumptions behind the worship experience than it does with the experience itself. These assumptions will determine whether the experience of worship—regardless of style or tradition—actually honors God and holds meaning for people. In light of this, at least two issues must be explored: seeker sensitivity and cultural relevance.[14]

Seeker Sensitivity

If the Bible calls believers to be thoughtful of irreligious people at their worship services, and God has historically blessed believers who gather together for corporate worship with evangelistic fruit, and the "front door" of the church has become the weekend worship service, then churches must rethink the level of seeker sensitivity their services display.

It is not difficult to think through what it would take to be sensitive—simply imagine how you would feel going into an alien worship environment.

My friend Bill Hybels often makes this point by encouraging people to imagine that their current neighbors have moved and a family of Buddhists has moved in next door. They're great people, though, and you soon forget about their religious orientation. Your kids play well together, you feel comfortable asking to borrow garden tools, and one vacation you return and find they've even mowed your lawn.

Opening the Front Door

- Seeker Sensitivity
- Cultural Relevance

One day while watching your sons play soccer on the neighborhood team, your Buddhist neighbor turns to you and says, "You know, Dan, you and Sarah are about the best neighbors we've ever had."

You say, "Sarah and I feel the same way about you guys!"

And then out of the blue, your new neighbor says, "Janet and I were wondering if you would do us a big honor. Would you try out the Buddhist temple with us this weekend? I know you're not Buddhists, and we're not trying to shove it down your throat, it's just that it would mean a lot to us if you would come just one time and see what it's like."

You are caught off guard and find yourself saying, "Sure, we'd be glad to come."

You get home and tell your wife, and she says, "You did what? We're going where?" You think of all the ways you might get out of it, but none seems to work without offending your new friends. So when the time arrives, the first thing you do is call and say you'll follow them over in your car. Psychologically, you already are wanting the security of an escape.

As you drive over, a thousand things run through your mind. You turn to your wife and ask, "You don't think they'll make us chant, do you? I don't think I even know how."

Your wife then turns and asks, "Do you think they'll ask us to sign anything or give our address? I don't want to end up on any kind of Buddhist mailing list!"

Then you say, "And what if we have to stand up and introduce ourselves? Somebody from work might see us and think we converted!" On and on the conversation goes, with the anxiety increasing as you get closer to the building. The bottom line is that you don't want to have to sing anything, say anything, sign anything, give anything, or do anything. Why do we forget these feelings when it comes to our church?

Growing in seeker sensitivity has nothing to do with devaluing authentic worship. It can be as simple as providing Bibles for those who don't have them or offering a degree of anonymity for first-time guests who don't wish to have their visit brought to everyone's attention. Simply imagine what it would be like to attend a service without the background or knowledge to know how to participate. When to stand, when to sit, what to recite, how to respond—this is unknown territory to a seeker. Seeker sensitivity has nothing to do with changing the church's message, just the church's manners.[15]

Cultural Relevance

In the spring of 1994, I taught at the Moscow Theological Institute. It was my first trip to Russia, and as you might imagine, I experienced a great number of differences between the culture of the United States and the culture of Eastern Europe. Particularly shocking was the way I was greeted by other men—with a kiss on the cheek! After my third or fourth kiss in a matter of minutes, I turned to my translator and said, "I guess kissing between men is normal here."

He laughed and said, "Yes, it takes a while to get used to it if you're from the West. If you don't want to be kissed on the mouth, just turn your cheek toward them when they lean toward you. If you don't want to be kissed at all, then simply take a step back and extend your hand." This was good news, since I hadn't experienced a kiss on the mouth yet!

I quickly learned that Russians express themselves differently in more ways than just the way they greet people. At the famed Moscow Circus and later at the Bolshoi Ballet, I discovered that applause is to be given in a rhythmic, united fashion. I was also soon conditioned to avoid sitting down before a meal. The practice with Christians is to stand for a prayer before eating. So whether it is affection, applause, or appreciation, my Russian friends express themselves in a manner appropriate to their culture.

The idea of cultural relevance can also be applied to worship, for it is about offering forms of expression that are meaningful to the worshiper. For God to be worshiped, Jesus taught that he must be worshiped in spirit and in truth; truth has to do with worshiping God in light of the full biblical witness about God, and spirit has to do with worshiping in a way that reflects the sincerity of our hearts (see John 4). Our tendency is to confuse tradition with orthodoxy and to make worshiping in "spirit" so privatized and individualized that there is little or no reflection upon cultural distinctives.

The irony is that many of our traditions that may now be irrelevant began in an effort to be relevant. For example, many churches meet for worship on Sundays at 11:00 A.M. The eleven o'clock hour was originally chosen to accommodate the milking schedule of dairy farmers. Yet long after the end of a predominantly agricultural society, many churches continue to meet at that hour—not because it is convenient, but because it now is perceived as something holy.[16] Similarly, the great hymns of Martin Luther are considered not only traditional, but sacred in their very form; but they were anything but traditional to the people of Luther's day. Many of the great hymns written during the Protestant Reformation, such as "A Mighty Fortress Is Our God," were based on barroom tunes that were popular during that period. Luther simply changed the lyrics and then incorporated the song into the life of the church. The result? People were able to express themselves meaningfully in worship.[17] Charles Wesley also borrowed from the secular music of his day, and John Calvin hired secular songwriters to put his theology to music, leading the Queen of England to call the songs "Geneva Jigs."[18] Bach provides a similar example, having used the popular cantata for weekly worship music. He was also known to seize tunes from "rather questionable sources and rework them for the church."[19] Even Handel's *Messiah* was condemned as "vulgar theatre" by the churchmen of his day for having too much repetition and not enough content.[20]

I read of one church leader who felt the situation with such musical efforts in his day had become dire. Hymns were being replaced in his beloved Baptist churches by more popular, contemporary tunes, and the use of the traditional hymnal was fading. He wrote, "For some years it has been apparent that the rage for novelties in singing . . . has been driving out the use of the old, precious, standard hymns. They are not memorized as of old. They are scarcely sung at all. They are not contained in the non-denominational songbooks, which in many churches have usurped the place of our old hymnbooks. We cannot afford to lose these old hymns. But the young people today are unfamiliar with them and will seldom hear any of them if the present tendency goes on untouched." Sound like a twenty-first century lament? Try 1891. The writer was Basil Manly, Jr., a founding professor of Southern Baptist Theological Seminary, who chose the preface to his own hymnal, *The Choice: A Selection of Approved Hymns for Baptist Churches*, as the place to voice his concern over the newfangled "gospel" song that had grown out of the Sunday school movement, camp-meeting revivals, and folk song traditions.[21] The point is that all music was, at one time, contemporary.

It should also be noted, as author Sally Morgenthaler reminds us, that to be culturally relevant does not involve having to throw out every piece of historic Christian communication.[22] There can be great appeal in the modern world through many traditional forms of worship, and indeed, there seem to be signs that this appeal is growing.[23] The point is that whatever forms of expression used must be meaningful to those who are attempting to use them to worship. If ancient forms of worship are used, they must be explained in contemporary ways. But the issue of cultural relevance is less about the undisputed value of the ancient and far more about the worth of the outdated. For example, classical music currently accounts for only 2 percent of the CD sales in the United States, while contemporary music accounts for nearly 90 percent.[24] Which style of music would help people worship best? For 2 percent of the population, it might very well be classical music. For 90 percent, however, a more contemporary form might better serve their efforts to worship God authentically. In fact, recent research on the most effective evangelistic churches in the Southern Baptist Convention reveals that the majority—43 percent—have either a contemporary worship style or at least a blend of the traditional and the contemporary. Only 1.5 percent were classified as "liturgical."[25] Yet rethinking worship in light of cultural relevance goes far beyond music; it speaks to everything from service times to the use of media, dress codes to terminology.

Cultural relevance, however, should never be confused with cultural accommodation. As Marva Dawn has written, the goal is "reaching out without dumbing down."[26] We live in what many would call a postmodern and post-Christian world.[27] The prefix *post-* simply means "after," intimating that we are no longer living in a world that is shaped by a biblical worldview. The values, morals, beliefs, and attitudes of today's culture are decisively non-Christian. Even the very idea of truth is challenged.[28] Consequently, cultural observer Kenneth Myers writes that the "challenge of living with popular culture may well be as serious for modern Christians as persecution and plagues were for the saints of earlier centuries."[29] Churches should be in the world but not of it. Unfortunately, this concern has led many to contend that when a church strives for any form of cultural relevance, the first step has been taken on the road to theological compromise.[30]

Certainly there are churches and leaders who have stepped outside the bounds of orthodoxy in their zeal for relevance, but to dismiss the importance of any relevance for the church on the grounds of possible compromise is far from warranted. The presentation of the gospel and the practice of worship cannot be separated from the culture in which they take place. While certain practices, such as the Lord's Supper and the reading and teaching of God's Word, are prescribed, there is freedom and diversity among churches in regard to many aspects of expression. As Richard Mouw observes, the incarnation itself is a profound exercise in divine "tailoring."[31] The goal that must be sought is relevance without compromise, not the dismissal of cultural relevance altogether. Offering contemporary forms of expression is vastly different from mindlessly embracing the values of the modern world. Christians must strive to connect the unchanging, uncompromising Word of God to the modern world.[32] While the message is timeless, the method is not, and we have confused traditionalism with orthodoxy far too long. The dynamic of the life of the church is not in the sacredness of cultural forms but rather in "the venturesomeness of participating with God in the transformation of contemporary cultural forms to serve more adequately as vehicles for God's interactions with human beings."[33]

Theologian Millard Erickson, building on the insights of William E. Hordern, offers a helpful distinction in the use of the terms *translation* versus *transformation*. Every generation must translate the gospel into its unique cultural context. This is very different from transforming the message of the gospel into something that was never intended by the biblical witness. Transformation of the message must be avoided at all costs. Translation, however, is essential for a winsome and compelling presentation of the gospel of Christ.[34] Charles Colson writes, "Many churches . . . have found the right balance; behind all the music and skits and fanfare stands a solidly orthodox message that deepens the spiritual life of the members. That is the key. What matters is not whether a church uses skits or contemporary music or squash courts. What matters is biblical fidelity."[35]

So when we speak of cultural relevance in regard to worship, it simply refers to translating the biblical forms and practices into expressions that have meaning to individuals in our modern world. As Donald P. Hustad, respected scholar and former organist for Billy Graham, noted, "Jesus did not give any instructions about what words or musical sounds or gestures or artwork should speak to us or for us. Evidently He (and the apostle Paul also) understood that modes of expression vary according to culture."[36]

The Essence of Worship

A man went to church with an angel as his guide. Every seat in the church was filled, but there was something strange about the service. The organist moved her fingers over the keys, but no music came from its pipes. The choir rose to sing, their lips moved, but not a sound was to be heard. The pastor stepped to the pulpit to read the Scriptures, but the man observing with the angel could not even hear the rustle of the pages. Then the Lord's Prayer was recited by the entire congregation, but not a single syllable was audible. The pastor went again to the pulpit, and the man could tell he had started his sermon as he gestured here and there to make his various points, but the man heard nothing.

Turning to the angel, the man said, "I don't understand. What does all this mean? I see that a service is being held, but I hear nothing."

The angel replied, "You hear nothing because there is nothing to be heard, at least not by heaven's ears. They are just going through the motions. Nothing they are doing has any meaning for them. Worship without the heart is not worship."[37]

If the act of worship is the expression of love and honor and praise to God, then it must be genuine and heartfelt; it must be meant. The more worship authentically reflects how a person naturally expresses those commitments and emotions, the more God-honoring it becomes. This is the heart of rethinking worship, for what is meaningful to one person may not be meaningful to another, particularly as vocabulary and style change over time.

6

Rethinking Structure

In the winter of 1988, nuns of the Missionaries of Charity were walking through the snow in the South Bronx in their saris and sandals looking for an abandoned building that they might convert into a homeless shelter. Mother Teresa, the Nobel Prize winner and head of the order, had agreed on a plan with Mayor Ed Koch after visiting him in the hospital several years earlier.

The nuns found two fire-gutted buildings on 148th Street, and the city of New York offered the buildings to the mission at one dollar each. The Missionaries of Charity set aside $500,000 for reconstruction. The plan was to create a facility that would provide temporary care for sixty-four homeless men. The buildings would provide a communal setting that included a dining room and kitchen on the first floor, a lounge on the second floor, and small dormitory rooms on the third and fourth floors. The members of the order, in addition to taking a vow of poverty, avoid the routine use of modern conveniences. As a result, the facility would have no dishwashers or other appliances, and laundry would be done by hand. For New York City, the proposed homeless facility was a godsend.

Then Mother Teresa's Missionaries of Charity encountered the bewildering world of bureaucracy. For a year and a half, the nuns, wanting only to live lives of service, found themselves traveling from hearing room to hearing room, presenting the details of the project. In September 1989, the city finally approved the plan and the Missionaries of Charity began repairing the fire-damaged buildings.

Then, after almost two years, the nuns were told that according to New York's building code every new or renovated multistory building must have an elevator. The Missionaries of Charity explained that because of their beliefs they would never use the elevator, which would also add $100,000 to the cost of the project. The nuns were told the law could not be waived even if the elevator would not be used.

Mother Teresa gave up. She did not want to devote that much extra money to something that would not really help the poor. According to her representative, "The Sisters felt they could use the money much more usefully for soup and sandwiches." In a polite letter to the city expressing their regrets, the Missionaries of Charity noted that the episode "served to educate us about the law and its many complexities."

As author and lawyer Philip K. Howard observes, no person decided to spite Mother Teresa. It was just the law. Yet he argues that the story of the Missionaries of Charity in New York reflects how rules can replace thinking. The result? What Howard calls "the death of common sense."[1]

The Critical Importance of Structure to the Church

The story involving Mother Teresa demonstrates how important the process of decision making is to ministry and how inhibiting bureaucracy can become. To make matters worse, a church's structure is often wedded to some of the most deeply rooted customs within the life of a church. Yet a church's structure is crucial when it comes to rethinking the church, because it is a church's structure that supports and facilitates the purposes and mission of a church.[2] Think of it functioning the way a skeleton serves a human body—it holds together and supports the working parts of the body to enable them to function as a body.

Consequently, a church's structure can either serve the church or bring it to a standstill. It can energize a community of faith or lead it toward ever deepening levels of discouragement. It can enable men and women to use their gifts and abilities for the kingdom of God or tie the hands and frustrate the most dedicated efforts of God's people. Why? Because the structure of any organization directly affects morale, effectiveness, and unity.

Morale

A major study of hundreds of organizations, including interviews with thousands of employees, discovered the leading "demotivators" that have a negative impact on morale. Leading the way were such issues as politics, unnecessary rules, poorly designed work, unproductive meetings, internal competition, discouraging responses to new ideas, inadequate use of potential, and overcontrol.[3] Structure dictated morale, and the type of structure that had a negative impact was one that did not treat people with respect. Traditionally, "companies define complicated rules, procedures, and guidelines to govern nearly every aspect of working life. These rules suggest to the employees that they are not trustworthy, lack common sense, and have even less capacity for making important decisions."[4]

**Areas Affected
by Church Structure**

- Morale
- Effectiveness
- Unity

111

Effectiveness

A second area directly affected by structure is effectiveness. During the late 1980s, reengineering swept the business world. *Reengineering* is the "radical redesign of business process for dramatic improvement."[5] When Michael Hammer first coined that term, he originally thought that the most important word in the definition was *radical*—the clean sheet of paper, the breaking of assumptions, the "throw-it-all-out-and-start-again" mentality. He writes that he has now come to realize that the key word in the definition of reengineering is *process*—a complete end-to-end set of activities that together create value for a customer.[6] Reengineering for true effectiveness, writes Hammer, has "deep and lasting *structural* implications" (italics added).[7] Structure works in an organization like grease on a wheel—it enables the working parts to operate smoothly and efficiently.

Unity

Unity can also be directly linked to structure. Most organizational designs attempt to provide support to a large number of people, activities, and resources. Therefore, structures have relational dynamics that can be either positive or negative. The giant of the computer industry, Microsoft, has made millionaires of hundreds of its employees. What is less commonly known is that many of these millionaires continued to work at Microsoft after they had achieved financial independence. This happened in spite of Microsoft's infamous sixty-hour workweeks and below-average perks. What would cause a bunch of millionaires, including a billionaire or two, to stick with it long after they had the financial independence to quit? Those who have studied such phenomena have concluded that it is the sense of community, and much of that community comes from a simple structure.[8] Rather than a structure in which the company is a machine and people are cogs, the structure is simplified and community-based, freeing up people to make their unique contributions. Bill Gates, chairman of Microsoft, said, "Individuals generate ideas, and Microsoft makes it possible for those ideas to become reality. Our strategy has always been to hire strong, creative employees, and delegate responsibility and resources to them so they can get the job done."[9] Result? A unity that keeps those who do not even have to work coming around.

Structure in Today's Church

Morale, effectiveness, and unity are key issues for the life of any church. Consequently, church structure must be evaluated in light of whether it promotes morale, effectiveness, and unity. There are a wide number of approaches to church government, from elder rule to a more congregationally based approach. Yet most forms of church government have three features that dominate their structure: committees, policies, and majority rule.

Committees

The work of the church is usually assigned to a network of committees. Most committees do not actually engage in ministry; rather, they are responsible for the oversight and administration of a ministry. They make decisions that others implement, or attempt to reach conclusions on issues that are then brought before the wider church for approval.

Certain committees, often called boards, are used to provide overall leadership and direction for the church. Such committees can be made up of elders, deacons, or other leaders, but the idea is that a small group of people provide oversight to the entire church.

Structure in Today's Church

- Committees
- Policies
- Majority Rule

Policies

Policies are written guidelines and rules that are intended to govern the decision making of the organization. They are designed to lay out a system of instructions and regulations that will ensure the proper running of a corporate machine. Most policies were created as a solution to a problem.

Majority Rule

The final feature present in the structure of most churches is some form of majority rule. Whether it is in the form of a monthly business meeting or simply how a committee or board makes a final decision, the raw democracy of majority rule is often employed.

Rethinking Structure

Even though committees, policies, and majority rule are deeply entrenched within the life of the church, it is important to note that none of the terms can be found in the Bible. The research of George Barna has discovered that the most successful churches subscribe to a singular philosophy: "The ministry is not called to fit the church's structure; the structure exists to further effective ministry."[10] Does the typical structure of a church serve the purposes and mission of a church? Increasingly there are concerns regarding committees, problems with policies, and misgivings about majority rule.

Concerns Regarding Committees

There are two concerns regarding committees and boards. First, committees take people away from the frontlines of ministry and move them into issues related to maintenance, such as budgets and organizational matters. Rick Warren observes that most churches take "their brightest and best people and turn them into bureaucrats."[11] Denominational executive Bill Hull likens it to a football game in which the first-string players are not on the field but rather taking tickets, selling programs, walking the aisles, working the refreshment booths, and counting gate receipts.[12] The result is that people become separated from ministry. They become involved not in the work of the church (ministry) but in church work (administration). "The more people you involve in maintenance decisions," writes Warren, "the more you waste their time, keep them from ministry, and create opportunities for conflict. Maintenance work also conditions people to think that their responsibility is fulfilled by simply voting on church business."[13] Warren argues that the difference between a committee and ministry is profound: "Committees discuss it, but ministries do it. Committees argue, ministries act. Committees maintain, ministries minister. Committees talk and consider, ministries serve and care. Committees discuss needs, ministries meet needs."[14]

Second, committees keep the people who are *doing* the ministry from making the decisions *about* the ministry. Authority and responsibility become distant from one another. This is a recipe for poor decision making, not to mention low morale. This is not to say that oversight—particularly in regard to vision, values, performance, and mission—are not appropriate. Yet the fact remains that the individuals who are the most intimately involved in a particular ministry are the best qualified to make the day-in, day-out decisions regarding that ministry.

The Problem with Policies

A policy governs decisions and directs procedure independent of a situation. In many ways, this is considered to be the strength of a policy. Yet as Philip Howard has observed, the one indispensable ingredient for the success of any human

115

endeavor is the use of judgment.[15] Policies are inherently limited because there can never be enough rules to cover every conceivable circumstance. A few years ago the federal government bought hammers with a specification that was thirty-three pages long. Howard asks, "Why not just trust the person to go out and buy hammers?"[16]

A second problem with policies is that they can become an end unto themselves. Rather than the policies serving the organization, the organization begins to serve the policies. "How things are done," writes Howard, "has become far more important than what is done. . . . Process now has become an end in itself."[17]

As an example, Howard cites the repair of the Carroll Street Bridge in Brooklyn, New York. Built in 1889, it was the nation's first retractable bridge. By the mid 1980s, it was in such disrepair that it could not carry traffic. In 1988 the city budgeted $3.5 million for an overhaul. Due to various procedures and policies, it was determined that bidding would take two years followed by five years for the work itself. But with the bridge's one hundredth anniversary coming up, Sam Schwartz, the deputy commissioner responsible for bridges, called in his chief engineer and asked him to draw up a repair plan, ignoring the contracting procedures. He also asked him to throw in architectural decoration, which was not part of the original repair plan.

Schwartz got the money and the contracts, and only eleven months later at a cost of $2.5 million, the bridge was fixed up in time for its centennial birthday. As a reward for completing the job in one-seventh of the time and at 70 percent of the budget, Deputy Commissioner Schwartz received an official reprimand.[18] As Howard observes, "The procedures Schwartz ignored—over thirty-five steps, involving six agencies and generally taking at least two years before any work can begin—exist to ensure complete neutrality and to protect against fraud. The fact that Schwartz was willing to stand up and take responsibility (and saved the city an estimated $1 million) was irrelevant. The ritual had been violated."[19]

It is no different with the church. Rick Warren writes, "We have imposed an American form of government on the church and, as a result, most churches are as bogged down in bureaucracy as our government is. It takes forever to get anything done."[20] This does not mean certain policies are not required to serve as guidelines and even as protection. Yet unhindered, policies can multiply to the point of organizational asphyxiation. George Barna simply asks, "Suppose your church had an opportunity to implement a ministry that had a high potential for positive impact, but needed to get started immediately. Could your church spring into action within hours or, at the most, a few days?"[21] Hopefully, the answer is yes. It takes trust for this structure to operate, but as Plato argued, good people do not need laws to tell them to act responsibly, while bad people will always find a way around law.[22]

Misgivings about Majority Rule

Majority rule is rooted in American democracy and, as a result, has often been incorporated unthinkingly into the church. The first misgiving about majority rule is noted by Yale University professor Marshall Edelson, who writes how an excess of consensus, or an overenthusiasm for democratic principles, can render an organization impotent in terms of actually doing anything.[23]

The second misgiving about majority rule, and one far more serious, is that the Bible teaches that a church is a family. (See Gal. 6:10; Heb. 2:10–12; 1 Peter 4:17.) In most family structures, the immature members (children) outnumber or at least equal the mature members (parents). In my family, there are two parents and four children. In the early years of our family, if we had voted on everything, we would have had ice cream for dinner every night, never have gone to bed, and taken up permanent residence at Disney World.

A church is a family and, as a result, contains members who are at different levels of spiritual maturity. If every decision is made by the majority instead of the most spiritually mature, then there is a very strong chance that the majority could mislead a church.

This is precisely what happened with the Israelites. Moses sent twelve spies into the Promised Land to report back to the people if it was everything God had promised. All twelve agreed that the land was flowing with milk and honey, but the majority said that the land could not be taken. Only two, Caleb and Joshua, were convinced that God wanted them to possess the land. The majority were allowed to rule, however, which left the Israelites wandering in the wilderness for another forty years.

A New Wineskin

Many structures can build morale, increase effectiveness, and stimulate unity. The Bible gives enormous freedom, requiring only that a church organize for effectiveness in regard to its purposes and mission. Two concepts, however, deserve serious investigation by any church interested in rethinking its structure: the separation of maintenance from ministry and the development of self-directed teams.

Separating Maintenance from Ministry

In most churches, the relationship between maintenance and ministry is simple: The pastors are the ministers, and the people are the administrators. "Being appointed, nominated, or elected to serve on committees is the primary form of lay ministry," observes William Easum. "Lay people see their primary leadership role to be 'running the church.'"[24] Yet this is diametrically opposed to the teaching of the Bible in relation to the pastor's role as equipper and leader, and creates a bottleneck for ministry.[25] Rethinking structure involves an entirely new paradigm: The people are the ministers, and the pastors are the administrators. As Rick Warren writes, "Maintenance is 'church work': budgets, buildings, organizational matters, and so forth. Ministry is 'the work of the church.'"[26] Easum adds that effective churches "believe that the role of God's people is to minister to people, in the world, every day of the week, by living out their spiritual gifts instead of running the church by sitting on committees and making decisions about what can or cannot be done."[27]

As a result, churches must decide whether they want to structure themselves for control or growth. Old forms of structure are designed for control. Rethinking calls for structuring for growth, which will result in high morale, effectiveness, and unity. For this to happen, both the pastor and the people will have to give up old and protected turf: The people must give up control of the leadership, and the pastor and staff must give up sole involvement in ministry. The pastor (or staff) has the responsibility to keep the church doctrinally sound and headed in the right direction, while the day-in, day-out ministry is fulfilled by the people who are actually being the ministers of the church.[28] This structural change also allows another important dynamic to be unleashed, which is the spiritual gift of leadership. Many structures handcuff leaders—particularly pastors and staff—from fulfilling their God-ordained and God-mandated charge to lead the church. This is not about opening the floodgates to an autocratic or dictatorial role for the senior pastor or any other leader, but it is about the critical importance of letting leaders lead.

Self-Directed Teams

Teams are indispensable to effective ministry and can be found throughout the Bible, from Nehemiah's strategy for rebuilding the wall of Jerusalem to the purposeful team building of Jesus with the disciples.[29] A ministry team is nothing more than a small group of people with a complementary assortment of gifts and abilities who are committed to a particular ministry that supports the purposes and mission of the church. And as Jon Katzenbach and Douglas Smith write in their book *The Wisdom of Teams,* "It is obvious that teams outperform individuals."[30]

But for a team to function at its optimal level of ability, the members must be self-directed, which means they must own the process or task at hand. Only when given the responsibility and the authority to follow through on a task can a team have the ability to become flexible and responsive to changing events and demands.[31] As Katzenbach and Smith note, self-directed teams "can adjust their approach to new information and challenges with greater speed, accuracy, and effectiveness than can individuals caught in the web of larger organizational connections."[32]

It should be noted that this does not mean that the team operates independent of the organization, much less its leadership and accountability structures. Michael Hammer likens it to how a football team operates. The offense and defense bring together a collection of tasks—blocking, tackling, passing, and receiving—that together achieve a result. The offense and defense operate within the confines of a carefully worked out game plan and strategy, but once a play begins, the players are largely self-directed. They have to be self-directed because the nature of the game demands it. When the ball is handed to a runner, it is up to him to determine whether to cut left, right, or go up the middle. While the offensive coordinator may have designed the play, selected the players, assigned them their roles, and even trained them, it is the players who are the implementers and who must have the freedom to make split-second decisions in light of the constantly changing realities of their situation.[33]

There is little doubt that mistakes will be made, and occasionally abuses will occur, but the gain through self-directed ministry teams will far outweigh any of the costs. And each mistake will only add experience to the team and increase its commitment to mutual accountability. I once heard of a man at IBM who made a mistake that cost the company over $10 million. The man immediately went to his supervisor in order to resign, but the supervisor said, "Are you kidding? We just spent $10 million educating you!"[34]

The Death of a Church

Church structure is important to fulfilling the purposes and mission of a church. Fred Craddock, longtime professor of preaching at Emory University, tells an interesting story about the first church he ever pastored. It was a small church in the hills of East Tennessee near what is now the Oak Ridge nuclear facility.

Craddock's time at the church coincided with the development of that great nuclear plant, so he witnessed the boom in population around this sleepy 112-year-old church. The region became filled with temporary workers setting up residence in RVs, tents, and makeshift shelters. Craddock saw it as a wonderful opportunity to reach out, so after church one Sunday he shared with some of the leaders how he wanted to start a campaign to invite all the new workers to their church. And then he began to hear it.

"I don't think they'd fit in."

"Are we sure that they're our type?"

"What kind of people are they anyway?"

"They're only temporary—they don't have houses or anything!"

Their conclusion? To take a vote the next Sunday. The day of decision came, and the first order of business was the following motion from the floor: "I move," said a man, "that to be a member of this church, you have to own property in the county." It was seconded, passed by the majority, and that ended that.

Years later, Craddock went to find that church. He wanted to show his wife the first church he had ever pastored and to see what had happened as a result of its fateful decision. He succeeded in finding the church building, but how it had changed! The parking lot, now freshly blacktopped, was full of cars along with RVs and vans, motorcycles and trailers. It was exactly as he had hoped the parking lot of the church might have looked so many years ago. But then he noticed the sign out front. No longer did it hold the name of the church. Now, in bright neon lights, it said, "Barbecue: All You Can Eat." It had become a restaurant. The church had died.

Craddock couldn't resist stating the first thought that entered his mind. He turned to his wife and said, "Well, it's a good thing this isn't a church anymore, or else all those people couldn't even be in there."[35]

Is your church's structure preventing growth, effectiveness, or unity? Few areas of church life are as important to rethink as structure. It may just keep your sign from one day reading "restaurant."

Rethinking Community

A few years ago I read a disturbing news story on the front page of a newspaper from Louisville, Kentucky. The headline read, "Church Meeting Ends in Fray, Beleaguered Pastor Resigns Amid Turmoil." The article told the story of the St. Paul Missionary Baptist Church, where years of discord, division, and turmoil finally erupted one Sunday into fistfights between members. It took over a dozen Louisville police officers to end the fray. The reporter had every right to be sarcastic when he wrote that those "who shortly before had been lifting hands in praise of God began raising hands against one another."[1]

We can relate this story and the less extreme stories of countless other churches to the story of the emperor's new clothes. Do you remember it? The emperor was deceived by two wicked men into believing that his imaginary clothes were real. As the weavers pretended to make the cloth, no one wanted to admit that they couldn't see it, for the men had said that only the very dull were unable to appreciate its beauty.

Soon everyone in the land had heard of the emperor's new clothes. A parade was scheduled, and people came from far and near. On the day of the parade, with flags unfurled and amid cheers, the emperor began the royal march through town. Having heard that only stupid people could not see the cloth, the townspeople began to praise the new suit. "The emperor's new clothes are wonderful," said one man. "Doesn't he look magnificent!" said another.

Then a little boy pointed at the emperor and began to laugh. "The emperor has nothing on!" he shouted. And then, as if a veil had been lifted from their eyes, all the townspeople began to laugh and shout, "Look, he has no clothes!"

Suddenly the emperor knew he had been deceived. Feeling very stupid—and very embarrassed—he ran and hid from the jeers and taunts of the crowd. Not until the boy said what was plain to see but people were afraid to admit, did anyone notice the problem.

This is the dilemma facing the modern church when it comes to the church and community. While the story of the St. Paul Missionary Baptist Church is extreme, deep division and discord are often present in the life of a countless number of churches. Even the unchurched do not want to attend because of the poor reputation churches have regarding the practice of community.[2] Yet no one wants to admit there is a problem. We are all afraid to say that the emperor has no clothes.

A Look in the Mirror

As a result, rethinking community in the life of a church must begin with a long, honest look in the mirror. There are certain things we may wish to see, much as the emperor wanted to believe he was fully arrayed in splendor, but there are telltale signs that often provide powerful witness to a more realistic assessment: an absence of authenticity, the presence of broken relationships, and a spirit of exclusion.

An Absence of Authenticity

The first sign that all may not be well in the area of community has to do with the absence of authenticity. In ancient Greece, all actors wore masks according to the characters they played. This is the basis for our term *hypocrite,* which literally means "mask wearer." Most people tend to think of a hypocrite as someone who says one thing and does another, concealing a secret life of sin that he or she hides under a veneer of spirituality. But the term can also apply to a person who wears a mask to conceal self. When the apostle Paul wrote to the church at Thessalonica, he said something very interesting: "We loved you so much that we were delighted to share with you not only the gospel of God but our lives as well" (1 Thess. 2:8). The word we translate as *life* is the Greek word *psuche,* which means soul. It refers to the very essence of a person. Hypocrisy means saying "fine" when someone asks you how you are doing, when you know you are not doing well at all. Instead of sharing your pain, your struggles, your heartaches, your anxieties, you interact with others in a superficial manner.

Problems with Community

- An Absence of Authenticity
- The Presence of Broken Relationships
- A Spirit of Exclusion

The Presence of Broken Relationships

A second sign to look for in the mirror has to do with the ongoing presence—and acceptance—of broken relationships.

During my seminary years, I was invited to serve as the senior pastor of a church just outside Louisville. To my surprise, they extended the invitation to me in spite of my age; I was only twenty-six years old. I soon found out why. I was their fifth pastor in less than ten years.

The church was full of division, discord, broken relationships, power plays, malicious gossip, and slander. Unsigned letters full of accusation and hate were commonplace. Deacons' meetings manifested a spirit that made the Inquisition look benevolent. Monthly business meetings felt like twelve rounds of boxing.

About a year after I became pastor and began to encounter the patterns of behavior that had plagued the church for years, I called some of the former pastors. I knew something was wrong. Was it me? Was it the church? I soon discovered the truth. The man who preceded me had suffered an emotional breakdown and had literally collapsed during a service. He was given a medical sabbatical, which he used to find another church. The pastor who served before him told me that he had been run off by a group in the church led by the man who was now the chairman of the deacons. According to this pastor, the deacon simply went to the parsonage one day and told the pastor that it was time for him to move on, and that if he didn't, he would make it so bad for him that he would have to leave. As I hung up the phone, my worst suspicions were confirmed, and for three years I lived in a nightmare.

When I tried to address the issue, both personally and from the pulpit, the response was amazing. The broken relationships, the fighting, and the divisions were not only seen as normal but as an inalienable right! One man actually said, "Why have a business meeting if we can't fight?"

A Spirit of Exclusion

Church members should also watch for a spirit of exclusion. Paul wrote, "May . . . God . . . give you a spirit of unity among yourselves as you follow Christ Jesus. . . . Accept one another, then, just as Christ accepted you" (Rom. 15:5, 7). Every church thinks it is friendly. Unfortunately, often church members are only friendly to each other, to people they like, or to people who are like them. That is not acceptance, much less community. Real acceptance involves looking at people, differences and all, and accepting them for who they are and how God made them. It doesn't matter if they are white or black, male or female, rich or poor.

The Church as Community

Rethinking community must begin with a clear understanding of what real community involves. As Bill Hybels has noted, the only kind of fellowship that most people have experienced at church has revolved around the fifteen or twenty minutes after the service when people stand around the church foyer and ask each other superficial questions.

"So how's it going at work, Jake?" one might ask.

"Fine, Phil. Say, you driving a new car?"

"Used," Phil replies. "What do you have going on this week?"

"Not much."

"Well, great fellowshiping with you, Jake."

"Same here."[3]

And that's about it—until the next week, when Jake and Phil will give it another round. But the Bible says that true fellowship has the power to revolutionize a life. True community is when the "masks come off, conversations get deep, hearts get vulnerable, lives are shared, accountability is invited, and tenderness flows. People really do become brothers and sisters."[4]

I was in Boston a few years ago and had the opportunity to do some sightseeing. I followed the famous "red line" through the heart of the city's historical district, went to the waterfront, the naval yard, and the commons. But what I really wanted to do was go to the Bull and Finch Restaurant and Bar. You may know it by another name—Cheers. The Bull and Finch was the inspiration for the hit TV series *Cheers*. While in Boston, I wanted to see the real thing. And I did. I went in, had lunch, and had a great time.

As I was walking out, I began to think about why people liked that series: the memorable characters, the funny stories, the great one-liners. But it clicked with me that what I liked most wasn't really the humor or the characters or the stories but something deeper. I liked the atmosphere, the relationships, the sense of community. Everybody seemed to care about each other, support each other, accept each other's weaknesses. It was the kind of place in which you'd like to hang out.

But Cheers pales in comparison to the truest, best, clearest picture of community that has ever been presented—the church as the new community. The second chapter of Acts presents a clear representation of the dynamics of community:

> They devoted themselves to the apostles' teaching and to the fellowship, to the breaking of bread and to prayer. Everyone was filled with awe, and many wonders and miraculous signs were done by the apostles. All the believers were together and had everything in common. Selling their possessions and goods, they gave to anyone as he had need. Every day they continued to meet together in the temple courts. They broke bread in their homes and ate together with glad and sincere hearts, praising God and enjoying the favor of all the people. And the Lord added to their number daily those who were being saved.
>
> Acts 2:42–47

In this portrait, we find that true community is where we can love and be loved, know and be known, serve and be served, and celebrate and be celebrated.

Love and Be Loved

Where there is authentic community, we can love and be loved. Luke observed that "they devoted themselves to the . . . fellowship" (Acts 2:42). The word Luke used for fellowship is the Greek word *koinonia,* which expresses companionship, sharing, and being intimately connected with another person.

It was an expression of enthusiastic love. People were taking the high road with each other, never assuming the worst or giving in to suspicion. True *koinonia* takes place when people are completely upheld, completely accepted, and completely supported.

Great risk accompanies this love, for it creates the opportunity for great pain and great hurt. Yet C. S. Lewis was wise to observe:

> **Marks of an Authentic Community**
>
> - Love and Be Loved
> - Know and Be Known
> - Serve and Be Served
> - Celebrate and Be Celebrated

To love at all is to be vulnerable. Love anything, and your heart will certainly be wrung and possibly be broken. If you want to make sure of keeping it intact, you must give your heart to no one, not even to an animal. Wrap it carefully round with hobbies and little luxuries; avoid all entanglements; lock it up safe in the casket or coffin of your selfishness. But in that casket—safe, dark, motionless, airless—it will change. It will not be broken; it will become unbreakable, impenetrable, irredeemable. . . . The only place outside Heaven where you can be perfectly safe from all the dangers . . . of love is Hell.[5]

While to love and be loved is never easy, it is an absolute necessity for authentic community. The main character of the classic children's book *The Velveteen Rabbit* is a little stuffed rabbit, all clean and new, who becomes "Real." During that process, the rabbit meets an old, worn-out, but very much loved, stuffed horse. Their dialogue captures the importance of a community giving itself over to love.

The Skin Horse had lived longer in the nursery than any of the others. He was so old that his brown coat was bald in patches and showed the seams underneath, and most of the hairs in his tail had been pulled out to string bead necklaces. He was wise, for he had seen a long succession of mechanical toys arrive to boast and swagger and by-and-by break their mainsprings and pass away, and he knew they were only toys, and would never turn into anything else. For nursery magic is very strange and wonderful, and only those playthings that are old and wise and experienced like the Skin Horse understand all about it.

"What is REAL?" asked the Rabbit one day, when they were lying side by side near the nursery fender, before Nana came to tidy the room. "Does it mean having things that buzz inside you and a stick-out handle?"

"Real isn't how you are made," said the Skin Horse. "It's a thing that happens to you. When a child loves you for a long, long time, not just to play with, but REALLY loves you, then you become Real."

"Does it hurt?" asked the Rabbit.

"Sometimes," said the Skin Horse, for he was always truthful. "When you are Real you don't mind being hurt."

"Does it happen all at once, like being wound up," he asked, "or bit by bit?"

"It doesn't happen all at once," said the Skin Horse. "You become. It takes a long time. That's why it doesn't often happen to people who break easily, or have sharp edges, or who have to be carefully kept. Generally, by the time you are Real, most of your hair has been loved off, and your eyes drop out and you get loose in the joints and very shabby. But these things don't matter at all, because once you are Real you can't be ugly, except to people who don't understand."[6]

Know and Be Known

Luke not only said that they were devoted to the fellowship, but that "all the believers were together and had everything in common" (Acts 2:44). They were sharing, talking, revealing; they were not holding anything back. The truth is that we all have weaknesses. True community takes place when we can stand up and say, "My name is John, and I'm an alcoholic," or "My name is Betty, and I have breast cancer," or "My name is Steve, and my marriage is falling apart," or "My name is Bill, and I have AIDS," or "My name is Carol, and I just lost my job," or "My name is Alice, and I'm lonely." The goal is to "take off our masks and be strugglers together, to weep and rejoice together, to be 'brotherly and sisterly.'"[7] When this happens, we open the door to the giving and receiving of love and support. Divorce, the death of a loved one, getting laid off, financial setbacks, miscarriages, cancer—people have walked through these things and have come out on the other end because of God's touch on their lives through a supportive community. If there is no authenticity, however, such community is not possible, because it begins with a willingness to admit weakness.

Author Robert Fulghum once reminded his readers of the childhood game hide and seek. Most of us played that game as children. There was only one problem—somebody always hid too well and nobody could find him. Sooner or later he would show up, mad because everybody had stopped looking for him. And then everybody would get mad at him because he wasn't playing the game the way it should be played. You have to be able to be found!

Fulghum then told of a doctor who discovered he had terminal cancer. He didn't want to make his family and friends suffer through his illness with him, so he kept his secret and eventually died. Everybody said how brave he was to bear his suffering in silence and not tell anyone, but his family and friends did not feel that way. They were angry that he didn't feel as if he needed them and didn't trust their strength. It hurt them beyond words that he didn't even say good-bye. Fulghum writes that this man hid too well.[8]

The church as the new community says, "Come on in, wherever you are. It's a new game. Hide and seek is over. It's time to be found."

To know and be known demands more than authenticity, however—it requires safety. The reason we do not share is because we fear what others will do with the knowledge they will gain. We fear betrayal, condemnation, and judgment. The cultivation of a community of safe people, therefore, must be maintained.

Serve and Be Served

The third mark of real community is that it is a place where one can serve and be served. When Luke described the early church, he noted that "selling their possessions and goods, they gave to anyone as he had need" (Acts 2:45). The early believers had a generous attitude, a spirit of giving to each other at their point of need.

I am a big fan of the Special Olympics, which features mentally and physically disabled athletes from around the world. One of the most memorable events that happened during the Special Olympics was a foot race among a group of people, each of whom had Down's syndrome. The runners were close together as they came around the track toward the finish line. One of them stumbled and fell. When that happened, the rest of the runners stopped. They went back as a group, helped the runner who had fallen to stand up, and then they all started running the race again.[9]

At Mecklenburg, our Home Teams, or small groups, flesh this out on a daily basis. They give people the opportunity to meet others, build friendships, and develop their relationship with Christ. A young couple became involved in one such group. The husband had come to Charlotte to start his own landscape maintenance company, and his involvement with the church and one of our Home Teams came during his company's start-up phase.

In working with a lawnmower one day, he had an accident. His hand got caught in the mower, and he lost part of it. That was bad enough, but then he faced the possibility of losing a lot more. He couldn't use his hand for several weeks, and he couldn't afford to hire extra help to perform his tasks. If the work didn't get done, he'd lose contracts and income, and his whole business could go under.

Then that young couple experienced a slice of community. Their Home Team pitched in and took turns doing his work for him. Men from his group got off work and went to work on a project, or they took a vacation day in order to go and serve him and his business. Because of his group's support, this man now leads a thriving business and holds a deeper understanding of God's design for the church. Such stories abound when community is in full vigor. I recall a single week when several events presented themselves to our church. First, a young couple in our church had a baby but had little or no support from their families. Then another young woman who had a husband and two young children was diagnosed with muscular dystrophy. Also, two sisters experienced the death of the man who had served as a substitute father to them, but they had no money to fly to the funeral. Finally, a young entrepreneur had to liquidate his business due to bankruptcy.

In most cases, these people would have had to face their situations alone. But here's what happened. When I visited the young couple in the hospital room, fourteen friends were present who had lined up child care and weeks worth of meals. The young woman who was diagnosed with muscular dystrophy received phone calls, visits, prayer, meals, and the raw emotional support she so desperately needed as she faced the frightening future of her illness. The two sisters were surrounded by people praying for them, supporting them, and listening to them as they grieved. They were also provided with complimentary tickets so that they could attend the funeral. The young entrepreneur had people in the church pray for him, encourage him, offer him jobs, and walk with him through his crisis.

Celebrate and Be Celebrated

Finally, authentic community is where we can celebrate and be celebrated. Notice how Luke ended his summary: "They broke bread in their homes and ate together with glad and sincere hearts, praising God and enjoying the favor of all the people. And the Lord added to their number daily those who were being saved" (Acts 2:46–47). They were in each other's homes, sharing meals, laughing and talking, enjoying life with each other and with God. It was so good that even people who weren't believers wanted to be believers because of the community. Dietrich Bonhoeffer expressed the same enthusiasm for community when he wrote that it "is grace, nothing but grace, that we are allowed to live in community."[10]

Building a Community

If we have looked in the mirror, seen the signs, and had our hearts touched by what a biblically functioning community can be, then the next step for rethinking is actually working toward bringing about that kind of a community.

Make Membership Matter

The first step we need to take toward forming a biblically functioning community is to make membership matter. The goal of membership in most churches is to define what it means to be a part of the community. This is accomplished by gaining an understanding of doctrinal and lifestyle issues and the overall purposes and mission of the church. Yet very few churches provide a class that outlines these issues as part of the membership process. This is like going out for a team and making the squad but never having to try out—or even to know what sport it is you're playing!

In the church of my youth, if you walked down the aisle, said you were a Christian and wanted to become a member, and agreed to be baptized (or simply said that you had been—nobody ever checked), then you were accepted by vocal acclamation. No class, no conversation or interview, no discussion of church structure, not even an explanation of the level of involvement that was expected. Your name was simply added to the roll. When this occurs, the distance between a church's membership and its actual attendance is vast. Though you would expect a church to have far more attendees than members, if for no other reason than the members would be in attendance along with invited friends and interested guests, in reality the number in attendance is less than the number on the membership list. For example, a typical Southern Baptist church in 1995 had 233 members but only 70 in average attendance.[11]

Building a Community

- Make Membership Matter
- Have a Clear Commitment to a Mission
- Have a Compelling Vision
- Value Community
- Work at Developing Community

What difference does this make to community? You cannot be unified as a community unless you have defined what that unity will be based on. Five things usually form the basis for uniting together as a church:

1. faith in Christ
2. values and beliefs
3. purpose and mission
4. strategy for achieving that purpose and mission
5. structure

If these five areas are not explained and protected through the membership process, there will be little hope for community.

As a result, many churches are moving to a process that makes membership matter. At Mecklenburg, newcomers' receptions are held throughout the year to give basic information about the church and its distinctives. Classes are then offered throughout the year to allow those interested in membership to learn about the church's vision, values, purpose, mission, and strategy (we call the class TeamLife). Next, interested persons meet individually with a small group leader or staff member to have all remaining questions answered in a personal way and to ensure that they are truly ready for membership. Do they subscribe to the church's doctrinal statement? Will they support the church's purpose, mission, vision, and values? Are they willing to be a fully participating part of the community? No one knows this about another person until he or she asks. When persons are ready to join the church, they sign a membership covenant (some churches have them walk down the aisle to formally enter into church membership). There could also be some type of public celebration at a service, through a newsletter, within a small group, or at an annual gathering.

Have a Clear Commitment to a Mission

In order to build community, a church also needs a clear commitment to a mission. Dietrich Bonhoeffer observed that the "more genuine and the deeper our community becomes, the more will everything else between us recede, the more clearly and purely will Jesus Christ and his work become the one and only thing that is vital between us."[12] Conversely, the more we make Jesus Christ and his work the most vital thing, the more genuine and deep will our community become.

In their research on the seven greatest teams of modern history—from Lockheed's top secret Skunk Works to the Walt Disney studio—Warren Bennis and Patricia Ward Biederman discovered that "groups seem to be most successful when undertaking tangible projects. . . . When the thing is finished, the group often spins apart."[13] Without a rallying point, a reason to be together, the group has no reason to be a group. Churches without a clear sense of purpose or mission don't often disband, but they do experience a breakdown in community. It is as if there is a certain amount of energy that comes from being together with others. That energy is either directed toward a common goal or cause or it turns inward and often results in conflict.

Have a Compelling Vision

The third ingredient for building a community is a clear vision for a biblically functioning community. A vision is an image, a picture, of what we are trying to do or become. When a vision for being the new community of the New Testament church is cast, then the first step toward becoming that new community has been taken.

Value Community

Church members must also value community. Something that is valued is celebrated, heralded, or applauded. When community-building attitudes and practices are rewarded and community-destroying mind-sets and actions are not, community takes hold and spreads. It is well known that what gets rewarded is what gets done. It is equally true that what gets honored is that which becomes pursued.

Work at Developing Community

The final component is simply the hard work needed to establish and maintain relational health. Any good marriage has been worked on, prayed over, and forged on the hard anvils of conflict resolution, truth telling, and sacrificial love. Community doesn't just happen. The Bible warns us of this when it counsels us in the area of relational health: "If a fellow believer hurts you, go and tell him—work it out between the two of you" (Matt. 18:15 MESSAGE).

I was on the phone with a woman on our staff. She had an idea that I didn't think too much of. I told her my opinion, we talked a little bit about it, and then we moved on. I didn't give it another thought until we talked again later in the day.

She called me back and said, "Jim, I just need to tell you that you hurt my feelings this morning. I had an idea that I liked, that I believed in, and the way you reacted made me feel stupid."

I was devastated. I loved the person who was talking to me, and the last thing I wanted to do was hurt her feelings. It hurt, it was difficult to hear, and it was difficult for her to say, but it was healthy. She could have sat on it and let it sour into bitterness. She could have let it drive a wedge between us. She could have called ten other people and said, "Boy, let me tell you what Jim said!" But she didn't. She practiced authentic community. In the context of love and commitment, she came to me to work it out.

Embodying such love and commitment will require that people be trained in the area of community. As mentioned in an earlier chapter, at Mecklenburg, this is built directly into our "Train" approach to discipleship, including the introductory "Training Camp" experience. We examine the nature of community as taught in the Bible, the importance and dynamics of truth telling and authenticity, and the biblical steps for conflict resolution. This training is important. Jesus said, "By this all men will know that you are my disciples, if you love one another" (John 13:35). Francis Schaeffer's comment on this is intriguing:

> Jesus is giving a right to the world. Upon His authority He gives the world the right to judge whether you and I are born-again Christians on the basis of our observable love. . . . Jesus is not here saying that our failure to love all Christians proves that we are not Christians. . . . What Jesus is saying, however, is that if I do not have the love I should have toward all other Christians, the world has the right to make the judgment that I am not a Christian. . . . There is a mark which, if the world does not see, allows them to conclude, "This man is not a Christian."[14]

This Is Church

It was a Wednesday night at Mecklenburg. The man walked to the podium on the stage and with shaking hands laid out the words he had written. He knew there was no way he could go through the next few minutes without them. They were precious words, written with many tears.

He stood before a church where he had served as one of the pastors, leading the music. With his wife looking on, he began, "I am here to tell you that I am sorry, so very, very sorry." And with those words, he began to share what the last nineteen months of his life had been like since he submitted his resignation for violating their trust.

He said that he wanted to come back—not as a pastor but just as a member of the church. He had sought forgiveness from God and now wanted to ask for their forgiveness as well. He had submitted to all that had been asked of him in regard to piecing his life back together, and now he wanted to take that final step. He returned because he could not stand the thought of being separated from those he loved and those who loved him. Community beckoned, and he was answering the call.

I walked up on stage, embraced the man, invited the man's wife to join him, and then said, "Not only do we welcome you back, we celebrate your return. We forgive you and simply stand with you as fellow strugglers."

And then, as people were invited to the platform to lay hands on the couple and pray for them and accept their return, a standing ovation broke out that seemed to never end. Then surrounded by people reaching in to lay hands on them for prayer, I remember blurting out the only words that seemed appropriate: "Now this . . . this is church!" And the applause began again.

And it was church, because it was a community where someone could love and be loved, know and be known, serve and be served, and celebrate and be celebrated. And everyone there knew the emperor had clothes and that here were Christians indeed.

8

From Rethinking to Change

American students who graduated from college in 2002 were born around 1980. They have no meaningful recollection of the Reagan era, and many do not even know he was shot. There has been only one pope, and they can remember only one U.S. president—Clinton.

They were eleven years old when the Soviet Union broke apart and do not remember the Cold War. They have never feared a nuclear war. *The Day After* is a pill to them, not a movie.

They are too young to remember the space shuttle *Challenger* blowing up, and Tiananmen Square means nothing to them.

Their lifetime has always included AIDS.

Atari predates them, as do vinyl albums, which means that the expression "You sound like a broken record" means nothing to them. They may have heard of an eight-track tape, but they've probably never seen one. The compact disc was introduced when they were a year old.

The original Star Wars movies look fake to them, and they would consider the special effects pathetic.

They have always had an answering machine for their telephone. Most have never seen a TV set with only thirteen channels, nor have they seen a black and white TV. They cannot fathom not having a remote control.

Roller skating has always meant in-line to them.

They never took a swim and thought of *Jaws*.

The Vietnam War is as ancient history to them as World War I. They have no idea that Americans were ever held hostage in Iran.

They can't imagine what hard contact lenses are.

They never heard the terms "Where's the beef?" "I'd walk a mile for a Camel," or "De plane, de plane!" Not only do they not care who shot J. R.; they have no idea who J. R. is.

And, of course, there has always been MTV.[1]

Strange, isn't it? And it goes to show how swiftly history moves on and how rapidly culture changes. But institutions are a bit different. There change comes a bit more slowly.

So how do we bring it about?

For most, the barrier is knowing what to fix, where to fix it, and what it looks like fixed. Hopefully, we have gained some ground there through the preceding chapters. The other major component is vision—coupled with a passion for the change to take place. I don't think you would have come this far in your reading if you didn't have that firmly in place. What is needed are practical ideas and principles and insights that can help navigate the waters. Entire books have been written on this matter, but here are some of the most critical ideas to keep in mind.[2]

Begin with Values

Jesus was quite clear in maintaining that new wine necessarily needs new wineskins. Thus new methods must be contained in new values. Indeed, the new values must come first. People need to be thoroughly converted and convinced as to the "why's" of change before the "what's" of change.

So how do you begin your value shift?

Begin with the foundational questions. Lead groups through them; make them the basis of a leadership retreat; walk through them as a church, answering them again as if for the first time. Don't even talk about methods—just talk about what you're about as a church, what your mission is, whom you're trying to reach, and what it means to be successful. Then you can get to the issue of strategy, the final foundational question.

Use this book as a starting point. I wrote *Rethinking the Church* to be used as a giveaway. Leaders can buy it and give it to their elders, deacons, church councils, and members to use in the process of rethinking, allowing for individual and group assessment as to where and how it might apply. This is why the book doesn't get into one particular model or a set of overly specific methods. Instead, it attempts to lay out the values and principles that serve as a road map for innovation and change, making it less threatening and more usable by leaders in widely differing contexts.

Another idea is to begin a series on the Book of Acts, recapturing a biblical vision for the values of the church. Also, take key leaders to select conferences that cast the vision in foundational terms. But begin with *values*, for they are the basis of everything. While Mecklenburg isn't facing the need for that kind of change or transition, we still give the book to new members, for whatever direction we will need to take in the future will be based on the values in the book.

Separating Methods from the Message

A second area that must be attended to for effective change is helping people not only see the values behind the change but to separate that change from their spirituality. The need is to help people understand that altering the methods doesn't necessarily mean altering the message. Most people initially confuse tradition with orthodoxy. Help them avoid making this common but critical mistake.

In his book *The Life You've Always Wanted,* my friend John Ortberg talks about our tendency to reduce our lives to what he calls identity or boundary markers—outward, superficial displays of vocabulary, dress, or style that tell the world who we are.

To be a hippie in the 1960s in the Haight-Asbury district of San Francisco meant driving a van plastered with peace signs and having long hair, a tie-dyed shirt, and granny glasses. In the 1980s, if you came across a BMW driven by someone with moussed hair wearing Gucci shoes and a Rolex watch and nibbling on brie, you would know you had spotted a yuppie.

We can reduce our spiritual lives to identity markers as well. These may be as faddish as fish stickers on our bumpers and WWJD bracelets on our wrists, or as deeply rooted as certain styles of music and dress for our services. These things tell us who we are; we make them signs of our spirituality.

In writing about this, Ortberg, one of the teaching pastors of Willow Creek Community Church, which is well known for its innovation, tells of a woman who once asked him whether he thought that the church where he worked might be worldly.

"What do you mean by worldly?" he asked.

"Well, you use drama, and people are used to that in the world. And you play contemporary music just like they're used to hearing. So how will they know you're any different? Everybody knows that as Christians we're supposed to be different from people in the world by being gentler and more loving, and everybody knows we're not. So don't we have to do something to show we're different?"

Ortberg thought to himself, *Let me get this straight—if we can't be holy, we should at least be weird?*

And that's how Christians often think.

Ortberg did not apply it this way, but consider this point: People's identity markers are often the very things we want to change as we apply our rethinking. Music, dress, and style are some of the things that come into play. When they do, we are often threatening people's very understanding of themselves as the people of God.

One of the keys to change, then, must be expanding the congregation's horizons on authentic spirituality—to move beyond superficial identity markers toward a true and dynamic relationship with Christ. On a practical level, this means helping people see beyond certain practices and rituals in regard to their understanding of the spiritual life.

The Five Groups—And What to Do with Them

A third thing we need to know about effective change is that it is not a monolithic enterprise, but multifaceted. At the very least, it involves five very different groups of people.[3]

First, there are the *innovators.* When it comes to change, these are the ones who tend to actually come up with the ideas that are at the heart of the rethinking. This group makes up about 2 percent of your church. Then you have the *opinion leaders,* the ones who communicate these ideas to the church. That communication may be either for or against the idea, but every church has a set of opinion leaders. In fact, they make up about 14 percent of the church. Together these two groups make up your community of leaders.

The next three groups are your followers. The first of the follower groups is the *early adopters.* They look to opinion leaders and tend to fall in line. When an idea is first presented,

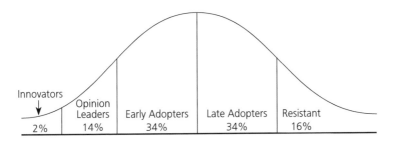

Innovators	Opinion Leaders	Early Adopters	Late Adopters	Resistant
2%	14%	34%	34%	16%

145

Dan will turn to Bob and say, "Bob, what do you think about this?" If Bob likes the idea, it will carry great weight with Dan. Bob is an opinion leader, and Dan is an early adopter. This group makes up about one-third of the church.

Then come the *late adopters,* who also make up about one-third of the church. These people are usually resistant to change until they are in the minority. Once the majority of the church is for an idea, the late adopters tend to go along for the ride. However, they do not usually fall in line right away. They like to put their finger to the wind and see which way the breeze is blowing.

The last group is the *resistant.* They don't want to change. The resistant feel that things should stay the way they are and that the church should do things the way it always has. These make up the last 16 percent of the church, but as any church leader can tell you, they can feel like a much larger force. They are a pivotal group, for they are as far from the leaders of the change—the innovators—as possible. But they are not necessarily bad people; they just get on board very, very slowly. Historically, this can be a good thing, for at times the resistant have kept the church from rushing into heresy. But when it comes to a change in methods, they will likely need personal attention.

A few things are worth noting about these groupings. First, your church really does have these five groups. Your church is not a monolithic organization that needs just one approach, or one strategy, to bring about change. It is made up of people, and people are complex. You have to be conscious of the dynamics of your congregation.

Second, this way of looking at things reminds us that change is very leadership intensive. It is not enough to come up with the idea; you have to *lead* your church through change, which means that you have to take the idea to the various groups of people within your church.

Look at the bell-curve drawing on page 145 and think of it as a process moving from left to right. It starts with the innovators, whose first job is to take the idea to the opinion leaders. This is critical, for if the opinion leaders get on board, they will influence the early adopters. Once keen to the idea, the early adopters will make those in favor of the change a majority. This will be of great significance to the late adopters, who often wait to see where the majority land.

And the resistant?

They must be tackled as best you can, one by one.

What is important to understand is that this process works like dominoes—push one over, and the rest fall into place.

To influence any of these groups will involve a conscious and ongoing investment in vision casting, one-on-one meetings, lunches—the hard work of bringing people on board with an idea. And not just with one of the groups, but with all five.

Understanding and Working: Two Continuums

A fourth insight about change is unique to those who want to make two critical but commonly joined changes: the change toward a more contemporary model of ministry and the change to become more outward-focused toward the unchurched. When approaching these two changes, it is important to remember that each has its own continuum.

First, there is the continuum of change from traditional to contemporary. This can include everything from contemporizing your worship service to updating your style of printing.

Traditional   >>>>>>>>>>>>>>>>>>>   Contemporary

The second continuum has to do with outreach—the move toward becoming a more outward focused church. Let's set this continuum up in terms of moving from seeker hostile toward ever increasing degrees of seeker targeted.

Hostile >> Indifferent >> Hopeful >> Sensitive >> Targeted

Several things about these continuums are worth noting. First, and perhaps most important, is that they are two distinct continuums, not one. It is very common for people to confuse the two, thinking that instead of two separate dynamics, they are one. As a result of this error in thinking, they mistakenly believe that in moving the church down one continuum—particularly from traditional to contemporary—they are also moving the church toward ever increasing levels of effectiveness with the unchurched, or becoming increasingly seeker targeted.

It doesn't work that way.

It is quite possible, and even common, for a church to be contemporary *and* seeker hostile. You do not lead your church toward a contemporary model alone and simultaneously achieve the full dynamic of what it means to become oriented toward reaching the unchurched. That is a separate continuum. Leading the church to substitute a praise band for the choir means very little in terms of your success at changing the front door of the church, much less its value system, toward the seeker who is the focus of outreach.

A second point worth noting is that the first continuum is much easier to navigate than the second one. Moving from traditional to contemporary is much easier than moving from seeker hostile, or even indifferent, to seeker targeted. This is because moving toward a contemporary model is mostly about style, not orientation.

The third lesson is more controversial but needs to be discussed. I have become convinced that there is a brick wall built onto the second continuum between the seeker-sensitive and seeker-targeted segments.

Hostile >> Indifferent >> Hopeful >> Sensitive >> Targeted

You can travel down the continuum from traditional to contemporary, and from seeker hostile all the way to seeker sensitive without much difficulty by using good leadership skills. Many churches have done so. I'm not saying it's easy, just doable. But what many churches are finding is that there is a barrier between the seeker-sensitive and seeker-targeted legs of the journey that blindsides them, and it is terribly difficult to move past.

I have spent a great deal of time reflecting on this, and I believe there are many reasons why change can run into roadblocks. But I have become convinced that this particular impasse is due to the nature of the change itself. You can move from traditional to contemporary and from seeker hostile all the way to seeker sensitive and never change whom the church primarily exists to serve. The customer who is being prioritized is the one who has always been prioritized—the believer.

Even a seeker-sensitive church is just that—sensitive—but the front door, the main services, the very orientation of the church is still predisposed to the already convinced. Consider a man who is more than willing to have contemporary music, casual dress, topical messages, and brand-new, relevant ministries. Not a problem. In fact, they serve him as much as they do a first-time guest. But you ask that same man to make a personal sacrifice, such as attending at another, less convenient time for worship, and the wheels come off, because suddenly it's clear—*the customer has changed*. No longer is he the one who is being prioritized. He is even asked to be inconvenienced for the sake of a new, and different, priority.

The wall is not impenetrable; it is just thick and tall. The key is knowing that it is there, looming before you. If you don't anticipate it, you will be blindsided in the way so many others before you have been. You will be moving down the continuum, arrive at the last and final step, see the promised land ahead of you and, if anything, speed the changes up even more—including the final customer change. Then the explosion that you were anything but prepared for will come.

This cannot be underestimated, for as you move closer to asking people to change their behavior or to change the actual culture, change becomes more difficult. Changing someone's knowledge is fairly easy; that just takes a change of mind. Changing an attitude is only marginally more difficult; that simply takes a change of heart. But to change someone's behavior takes a change of lifestyle, and to change an institution's behavior takes a change of culture, and those are huge shifts.

The Four Steps of Change

Understanding the actual steps of change is important. The first and most important step is to pray and pray hard. But that is a given. Beyond that, four critical steps must be taken.

1. Establish a Sense of Urgency

People will not even consider change unless they are impacted on an emotional level. Leadership expert John Kotter of Harvard says that if change is not considered necessary, people "will find a thousand ingenious ways to withhold cooperation."[4] A perceived problem or need must be generating a certain amount of emotional energy. For the change agent, or agents, one of the keys to this is passion: If you don't seem to care, they won't bother to care. Note that this is more than simply articulating the logic of a particular set of actions. People must be communicated with on an emotional level. A sense of urgency must be conveyed. The Bible reminds us that we are transformed through the renewing of our mind (Rom. 12:2). So whatever the change may be, be sure to convey what the stakes are and why the change is so important.

For example, why should anyone contemplate evaluating a weekend service in light of its effectiveness in communicating the truth of Christ to a lost person? If church members do not perceive that lost people matter or perceive that they are being reached quite well through current approaches, then any change that might be suggested will die at the starting gate. Change leaders must communicate the importance of those apart from Christ and the exact state of the church in current effectiveness at reaching them. It is up to the leader to say, "We will stand before God one day and give an account for our lives. And this generation of Christians is responsible for this generation of non-Christians. God will ask, 'Did you do all that you could? Did you match the intensity and fervor I brought to the cross?'" People must be brought to the point of understanding that it would be a tragedy if change didn't happen. They must not simply embrace change, but cry out for it.

2. Develop and Cast a Compelling Vision

Where is this change going to take us? What will it mean for us? What difference will it make? Paint the picture for people of what the change will actually *do*. Vision is nothing less than the language of leadership. It points the way, it motivates people to take the steps needed to get there, and it coordinates the actions of all involved. At its best, it paints a simple but compelling picture of a better tomorrow in ways that appeal to everyone's interests.

This has to be more than a single motivational talk. In reality, not only does vision leak, but it gets lost in the competing noise for attention. Consider a business example. The total amount of communication going to the typical employee in an American company in a three-month period is 2.3 million words or numbers. The typical communication of a change vision over the same period has been calculated at 13,400 words or numbers (the equivalent of a single thirty-minute speech, coupled with a one-hour-long meeting, a six-hundred-word article in the firm's newspaper, and a two-thousand-word memo). Thus the change vision captures only .58 percent of the communication competing for the average employee's attention. This is akin to a gallon of information dumped into a river of dialogue.[5]

Vision must be repeated over and over again. When both you and the core change agents are sick of hearing it, then you might be approaching some degree of connecting with the group at large. The point is that one message, or even one cluster of messages, simply isn't enough. People's grasp of the vision fades fast, and it must be continually cast—and not simply to one group, but to all groups, and it must be cast in all settings—in one-on-one sessions; to committees, boards, and ministries; during weekend services; over lunches and breakfasts. Use articles, stories, facts, statistics—any simple, to-the-point method tied to the values behind the change. And communicate over and over again. You cannot overcommunicate.

3. Begin Implementation

After the vision casting eventually pays off in consensus and approval with the various groups in the church, begin implementing the change. While seemingly obvious, there is a tendency within all of us to hold off on actually pulling the trigger. Yet clear start dates, with real manifestations of the goal at hand, are decisive.

4. Give Progress Reports

Let everyone know how the change is doing. The war is not won simply with implementation. The question then becomes whether or not the change should be maintained. Rick Warren has written from many years of experience that "vision and purpose must be restated every twenty-six days to keep the church moving in the right direction."[6] Whether monthly is too much or too little, it must certainly be ongoing. So let people know what is happening. Talk about successes and breakthroughs. Let people see and feel the benefits that are flowing from the change.

Something to Remember

One of the most important insights to remember is that change takes time. Don't overestimate what you can do in a year, but don't underestimate what you can do in ten. A lack of patience has caused many church leaders to get into trouble that would have been easy to avoid. As change agents, they get in a hurry and begin implementing changes that people simply aren't committed to, much less emotionally prepared to experience. Thus resistance comes—not just from the "resistant," but from early adopters and even opinion leaders.

The Limits of Change

Another reminder has to do with the limits of change. No matter how strong your vision or how well the change is led, it may not take.

And there are several reasons why.

To begin with, it may not be God's will for your church to change in a particular way. The vision and the passion of the innovators—and even the opinion leaders—may not be God's will for the church. As a result, the Holy Spirit may not open up the doors of change for you.

Another reason change may have limits is because of the barriers that may exist for certain changes, such as the brick wall between a seeker-sensitive approach and a fully seeker-targeted approach. There are many such barriers, and they can be very difficult—if not impossible—to break through independent of a church plant.

A third reason for limits flows from the reality that the greater the change, the greater the leadership level required for the change. If you are a "small *l*" leader, but you're trying to strap on a "capital *L*" level of change, you may be limited as to what you can pull off.

Finally, you may be limited in regard to the amount of change by a spirit in your church that resists the work of the Holy Spirit. This is a bit dangerous to explore, much less to offer, as it is easy and tempting to assume at the first sign of resistance. Yet it cannot be denied that some churches have very hardened hearts and spirits. You simply cannot read the seven letters to the seven churches in Revelation, much less the apostle Paul's many epistles, without realizing that different churches have different characters and levels of maturity in relation to the work of the Holy Spirit. You may reach a point at which you have changed a church as far as it can be changed. If God is calling you to a deeper level of change, then you may need to consider going to another church or even starting a new one.

Character Traits of Change Agents

When it comes to change, one of the least talked about—but possibly most important—issues is the character traits of the change agents themselves. What are these character traits?

The first is courage. A few years ago I was speaking at a conference about some of the innovations marking the most effective churches of our day—approaches to evangelism, ministry, and structure the Holy Spirit is using to bring about renewal, revival, and astounding fruit.

A pastor came up to me afterward, pulled me aside, and said, "I know that everything you said today is right. It's true. It's the only hope of the church. But I need to be honest with you. I'm a few years away from retirement, and I'm simply not willing to deal with the conflict and controversy, division and discord it might bring."

Can you empathize?

Who in ministry couldn't? But I believe that when he said that to me, heaven wept. Ministry is not for the limp-wristed. It is not for the weak at heart. It is not for those who are seeking a safe, calm, conflict-free life. It is for those willing to do whatever it takes.

Theodore Roosevelt once said:

> It is not the critic who counts, not the man who points out how the strong man stumbled, or where the doer of deeds could have done them better. The credit belongs to the man who is actually in the arena; whose face is marred by dust and sweat and blood; who strives valiantly; who errs and comes short again and again; who knows the great enthusiasms, the great devotions, and spends himself in a worthy cause; who, at best, knows in the end the triumph of high achievement; and who, at the worst, if he fails, at least fails while daring greatly, so that his place shall never be with those cold and timid souls who know neither victory nor defeat.[7]

The second character trait that change demands is determination. The apostle Paul made the impact he made because he was determined to make the impact he made. It would be difficult to read his writings and not see raw determination coursing through his veins. He wrote of running the race, finishing well, beating his body, and going for the prize.

I heard someone talk about going to the United Center in Chicago to watch Michael Jordan and the Chicago Bulls play a basketball game. They had received a special invitation to arrive early and tour the building. They saw something interesting. Forty-five minutes before the practice and shoot-around scheduled by the coach, Michael Jordan, the greatest basketball player who has ever played the game, was on the court practicing. Apparently there was a facet of his game he felt needed some fine-tuning.

No one made Jordan do that—just Jordan. But it was that kind of determination that led him to make such an impact on the court.

Or consider Gary Player, who won more international golf tournaments in his day than anyone else. When Player was competing in a tournament, people often would approach him and say, "I'd give anything if I could hit a golf ball like you."

On one particularly tough day, Player was tired and frustrated. Once again, he heard the comment, "I'd give anything if I could hit a golf ball like you."

Player's usual politeness failed him as he replied, "No, you wouldn't. You would give anything to hit a golf ball like me if it was easy. Do you know what you've got to do to hit a golf ball like me? You've got to get up at five o'clock in the morning, go out on the course, and hit one thousand golf balls. Your hand starts bleeding, and you walk up to the clubhouse, wash the blood off your hand, slap a bandage on it, and go out and hit another one thousand golf balls. That's what it takes to hit a golf ball like me."[8]

Those who experience the fruit of change pay a price, and the payment is largely in the form of persistence. They stay with it, and over the course of time, achieve the vision longed for.

Conclusion

I remember trying out for the basketball team in high school. I made the team, but trying out was something of an experience. On the first day of tryouts, the coach ran a scrimmage. When I finally got my chance to go into the game, I was pumped. On the very first play, I intercepted a pass, took the ball the length of the court, "skyed" over every other player, and made the prettiest layup you ever saw.

The coach blew the whistle, stopped the game, and called me over to the bench. I was walking ten feet off the ground. I just knew my shot was so good that he had to stop the game just to tell me!

I got to the sideline, and he said, "White, that was a great shot. You went to the wrong basket, but it was a great shot!"

The issue for any organization, including the church, is not how pretty the layup is, but whether it is made at the right basket. In other words, the issue is not the efficiency of the church, which is doing things right, but its effectiveness, which is doing the right things. This has been the theme of the book. The church must rethink its current processes in order to determine if it will effectively fulfill the Great Commission. As the ancient Chinese proverb says, "If we do not change direction, we are likely to end up where we are headed."

The church is far more than a human enterprise that rises or falls on the management and organization we bring to its efforts. All our efforts are worthless apart from the energizing presence and power of God. (See Ps. 127:1.) Yet we must avoid a pious irresponsibility that produces passive believers who, as Rick Warren says, "use spiritual-sounding excuses to justify a church's failure to grow."[1] The balance is found in Proverbs 21:31: "The horse is made ready for the day of battle, but victory rests with the LORD." Victory rests with God, but we must prepare the horse to the best of our abilities.

Rethinking may mean that the church has to change. Difficult as this may be, it is absolutely essential. It will prove ruinous if the church allows itself to maintain a business-as-usual approach. George Barna likens the church to a frog in a kettle of water. He notes that if you place a frog in a kettle of water and then begin to raise the water's temperature slowly, the frog will continue to remain in the water, even to the boiling point. Because the temperature is increased gradually, the frog does not sense it is in danger and stays in the water until its death. "Like the frog," writes Barna, "we are faced with the very real possibility of dying because of our unresponsiveness to the changing world around us."[2]

The change a church undergoes, however, cannot be merely cosmetic. A Search Institute study on public school reform efforts since 1985 illustrates that there are two approaches to change. In their research report, Peter Benson and Carolyn Elkin write that "schools have taken two different approaches to change. One approach is called 'tinkering,' in which schools attempt to increase effectiveness by adding one or two new program features without modifying the underlying educational assumptions, structure and format. The other approach is called 'restructuring,' in which schools introduce new models of teaching and learning." Their conclusion is critical: "The national effort to reform schools has largely failed because most schools have opted for tinkering."[3] No wonder a study by the South Carolina Baptist Convention found that the fastest-growing churches were the ones most willing to move beyond tinkering and enter into real and substantive change. In fact, 80 percent of growing Southern Baptist churches did such things as make changes in their music or create new small group ministries.[4]

At the same time, change does not have to mean compromise. Interestingly, even such a dispassionate observer as the *Atlantic Monthly* noted that innovative churches "may be market-driven, culturally sensitive, and cutting-edge, but this does not make [them] 'progressive' or 'liberal' on the fundamentals."[5] Author and pastor Gene Getz reminds us that this was the pattern for the New Testament church. He notes that what the early Christians said was consistent; the way they said it and how they went about such things as ministry or evangelism varied from situation to situation. They considered the directives as absolute, but their methods were relative and merely served to accomplish divine ends.[6] There is no reason this first-century paradigm cannot continue to operate in the church of the twenty-first century.

But there has been a secondary theme to this book that has been somewhat more reserved in its presentation. Along with a rethinking of processes, the church must rethink its attitude.

In Greek mythology, Narcissus was the character who, upon passing his reflection in the water, became so enamored with himself that he pined away until he was transformed into the flower that bears his name. From this story comes the term *narcissism*, which refers to a mentality that places personal pleasure and fulfillment at the forefront of all concerns.

I fear that the contemporary church has become marked by a narcissistic attitude that places the individual needs and desires of the believer at the center of attention.[7] Much like the older brother in Jesus' story of the prodigal son, believers often act as if the fattened calf should be reserved for them and them alone. The attitude is that the church exists for me and my needs; I do not exist for the church and its needs. As a result, the desire is not to learn how to feed ourselves, much less to feed others, but to be fed. Ministry is that which happens to us, not something that we make happen for others. Worship is evaluated by what we get out of it, not by what we give to God through it. Unless confronted, this attitude will inhibit the growth and effectiveness of the church far more than even the most archaic and dysfunctional of processes. And this may involve the greatest rethinking of all. As Henri Nouwen observed about the elder brother in Jesus' story of the prodigal son, "the hardest conversion . . . is the conversion of the one who stayed home."[8]

Yet the conversion must take place. Professor Robert Coleman said it best when he declared that we "are not called to hold the fort, but to storm the heights."[9] The church is on a mission; it has a cause. The purpose of the church is to fulfill the Great Commission. We do not grow in Christ for our own sake, but for the sake of the cause.

For the Sake of the Cause

The most enduring image of the Centennial Olympic Games in Atlanta was that of a four-foot, nine-inch, eighty-seven-pound gymnast named Kerri Strug being carried by her coach to the medal platform to receive her gold medal along with the rest of her team. What led up to this moment was drama at its highest.

The American women's gymnastics team held a thin lead over the Russians, and the contest had come down to the last event, the vault. The first four women on the U.S. team did well, but then the fifth member of the team faulted her landing on both attempts. Because the team could only discard the lower of the two scores, Kerri became the key to winning the event and, because the vault was the last apparatus, the key to winning the gold medal.

On her first effort, Kerri suffered a fall. The entire crowd grew silent, sensing the medal slipping away. But it was worse than a poor first try. Kerri had twisted her ankle, tearing two ligaments. She didn't know whether to go for it, but in the end, she said she just whispered a little prayer, asking God to help her out somehow.

Repeating "I will, I will" to herself, she charged down the runway, vaulted, twisted through the air, and then landed on an ankle so badly sprained that it could only hold her upright for a second. But that second was long enough for her to guarantee the first Olympic gold medal ever won by an American women's gymnastics team. She scored one of the highest scores of the meet.

When it became known what she had done and people saw that she had to be carried to the platform, even the men became misty eyed. When asked why she did it, she expressed her commitment, not just to the competition, but to the team. They were on a mission, and she wanted to play her part.[10]

This is the attitude that must be recaptured for the church—people willing to step up to the plate, to become part of something larger than themselves, something that will live on for eternity. The church is the hope of the world, and unless we rethink our processes and, more importantly, our attitude, we will lose this generation for Christ.

One of the great scholars of the Renaissance, Erasmus, told a mythical tale about Jesus' return to heaven after his time on earth. The angels gathered around him to learn what had happened. Jesus told them of his miracles, his teaching, and then of his death and resurrection.

When he finished, Michael the archangel asked, "But Lord, what happens now?"

Jesus answered, "I have left behind eleven faithful men who will declare my message and express my love. These faithful men will establish and build my church."

"But," responded Michael, "what if these men fail? What then?"

And Jesus answered, "I have no other plan."[11]

There is no other plan outside the church for God's redemptive work. It rests in our hands and in our hearts. Let the rethinking begin, and begin now.

Notes

Preface

1. It was the research by Michael Hammer and James Champy in *Reengineering the Corporation* and Michael Hammer's work in *Beyond Reengineering* that first encouraged me to use such ideas in regard to the church. Readers of those books will recognize a similarity between my definition of *rethinking* and Hammer and Champy's definition of *reengineering*.

Introduction

1. As noted in *Current Thoughts and Trends* 12, no. 5 (May 1996): 8.

2. Michael Hammer and James Champy, *Reengineering the Corporation: A Manifesto for Business Revolution* (New York: HarperBusiness, 1993), 1.

3. Ibid.

4. Ibid., 10.

5. Ibid., 30.

6. Ibid., 17.

7. Leith Anderson, *Dying for Change: An Arresting Look at the New Realities Confronting Churches and Para-Church Ministries* (Minneapolis: Bethany, 1990).

8. Statistics compiled by Les Parrot III and Robin D. Perrin, "The New Denominations," *Christianity Today*, 11 March 1991, 29. A 1994 report revealed that few of the ten largest U.S. denominations reported membership increases or drops of more than 1 percent. On this, see *The Yearbook of American and Canadian Churches 1994*, as reported in *National and International Religion Report* 8, no. 8 (4 April 1994): 3.

9. Ken Garfield, "Some Churches Losing Members," *The Charlotte Observer*, 30 March 1996, 2G.

10. "Religious Congregations and Membership in the United States: 2000," sponsored by the Association of Statisticians of American Religious Bodies and published by Glenmary Research Center.

11. This has been the case since at least 1991, as noted in the *SBC Handbook* (Nashville: Convention Press, 1991), produced by the Church Administration Department of the Sunday School Board of the Southern Baptist Convention. Figures taken from the 1994 Annual Church Profile reveal that 49.5 percent of all SBC churches plateaued and 20.2 percent were in actual decline. The recent growth rate is still well below the pace of U.S. population growth according to the report "Religious Congregations and Membership in the United States: 2000," sponsored by the Association of Statisticians of American Religious Bodies and published by Glenmary Research Center.

12. As reported by Mark A. Kellner, "Flock Strays from U.S. Churches," special to the *Washington Times*, at www.washtimes.com.

13. These figures were cited in *The Win Arn Growth Report*, no. 32, 2.

14. *The Pastor's Weekly Briefing* 3, no. 42 (20 October 1995).

15. Barna, *Index of Leading Spiritual Indicators*, 109.

16. From the *Executive Summary of A Report on Religion in the United States Today* (Hartford, Conn.: Hartford Institute of Religious Research, 2001).

17. George Barna, *The State of the Church 2002* (Ventura, Calif.: Issachar Resources, a Division of the Barna Research Group, Ltd., 2002), 112.

18. "Attendance Drops," *The Charlotte Observer*, 9 March 1996, 2G. An earlier report found that Sunday school and small groups were also shrinking in attendance. On this, see George Barna, *Virtual America: The Barna Report 1994–1995* (Ventura, Calif.: Regal, 1994), 46–53.

19. Katy McLaughlin, "The Religion Bubble: Churches Try to Recapture Their 9/11 Crowds," *The Wall Street Journal*, 11 September 2002, D1.

20. Barna, *State of the Church 2002*, 12.

21. Ibid., 17. The unchurched here are defined as those who have not attended a Christian church service during the past six months other than for special events such as weddings or funerals.

22. *World Christian Encyclopedia*, ed. David B. Barrett (Oxford: Oxford University Press, 2001).

23. The survey was performed by the Barna Research Group, Glendale, Calif.

24. "Spirituality Returns," *Swing* (March 1996).

25. Barna, *Leading Spiritual Indicators*, 5.

26. Robert C. Fuller, *Spiritual but Not Religious: Understanding Unchurched America* (Oxford: Oxford University Press, 2001).

27. Wade Clark Roof, *Spiritual Marketplace: Baby Boomers and the Remaking of American Religion* (Princeton: Princeton University Press, 1999), 85.

28. If you surveyed your community, you might get different answers. Yet these responses—from a city with a relatively traditional Bible Belt culture—mirror the results of similar studies by churches from Chicago to Los Angeles. For example, both Saddleback Valley Community Church in

Mission Viejo, California, and Willow Creek Community Church in South Barrington, Illinois, discovered virtually identical responses. See Rick Warren, *The Purpose Driven Church* (Grand Rapids: Zondervan, 1995), 188–92; and Lynne and Bill Hybels, *Rediscovering Church* (Grand Rapids: Zondervan, 1995), 57–59.

29. The illustration of the Swiss watchmakers has been adapted from Joel Barker, *Future Edge* (New York: William Morrow, 1992), 15–19.

30. Churches have adapted with varying degrees of faithfulness to the Christian faith, to be sure. Whether faithful adaptation or heretical adaptation, however, it has been adaptation that has saved the church. On this, see Nathan O. Hatch, *The Democratization of American Christianity* (New Haven: Yale University Press, 1989); and R. Laurence Moore, *Selling God: American Religion in the Marketplace of Culture* (New York: Oxford University Press, 1994).

Chapter 1: Rethinking the Foundational Questions

1. Taken from Doug Murren, *LeaderShift* (Ventura, Calif.: Regal, 1994), 70.

2. As quoted by Roger Dow and Susan Cook, *Turned On* (New York: HarperBusiness, 1996), 6. Interestingly, *Sports Illustrated* agrees, recently launching an all-sports network with CNN.

3. A similar set of questions is at the heart of the sweeping reengineering taking place in the business world, and examining them may be helpful. On this, see James Champy, *Reengineering Management* (New York: HarperBusiness, 1995).

4. Adapted from Chuck Colson and Jack Eckerd, *Why America Doesn't Work* (Dallas: Word, 1991), xii.

5. Allan Cox, with Julie Liesse, *Redefining Corporate Soul: Linking Purpose and People* (Chicago: Irwin, 1996), 3.

6. Warren, *Purpose Driven Church*, 95–109. Other helpful books on the nature and purpose of the church include Charles Colson, *The Body* (Dallas: Word, 1992); Avery Dulles, *Models of the Church*, 2d ed. (Garden City, N.Y.: Doubleday, 1974); Gene Getz, *Sharpening the Focus of the Church* (Wheaton: Victor, 1984); Kevin Giles, *What on Earth Is the Church? An Exploration in New Testament Theology* (Downers Grove, Ill.: InterVarsity Press, 1995); and Charles R. Swindoll, *The Bride* (Grand Rapids: Zondervan, 1994).

7. Adapted from John C. Maxwell, *Developing the Leader within You* (Nashville: Thomas Nelson, 1993), 25–26.

8. From the *Executive Summary of A Report on Religion in the United States Today*/2001.

9. Lewis Carroll, *Alice's Adventures in Wonderland* (New York: Alfred A. Knopf, 1984), 89.

10. George Barna prefers the term *vision* for this discussion. On this, see his two books *The Power of Vision* (Ventura, Calif.: Regal, 1992) and *Turning Vision into Action* (Ventura, Calif.: Regal, 1996).

11. George G. Hunter III, *Church for the Unchurched* (Nashville: Abingdon Press, 1996), 36–41.

12. Ibid., 42.

13. Warren, *Purpose Driven Church*, 82. Interestingly, Arn asked the same question of the pastors of those churches. The results were the opposite: 90 percent said the church exists to win the world; 10 percent said the church exists to meet the needs of the members. This dilemma is not unique to churches. The Murdock report surveyed about eight hundred laypeople, pastors, and seminary professors and discovered disagreements about the mission of seminary education. When asked to rank the top five abilities seminary graduates needed to possess to minister effectively, pastors and laypeople felt that theological knowledge ranked last in importance, while seminary professors felt it should be first. On this, see Timothy C. Morgan, "Re-Engineering the Seminary," *Christianity Today*, 24 October 1994, 74–78.

14. See Al Ries, *Focus: The Future of Your Company Depends on It* (New York: HarperBusiness, 1996).

15. Michael Treacy and Fred Wiersema, *The Discipline of Market Leaders* (Reading, Mass.: Addison-Wesley, 1995), 199.

16. Quoted in Marc Spiegler, "Scouting for Souls," *American Demographics* 18, no. 3 (March 1996): 46.

17. Churches that are homogenous in nature have often been criticized, as if the ideal for every local church is the complete integration of every possible race, creed, and disposition. This is not only nonbiblical in regard to the makeup of the various New Testament churches, it is virtually impossible in regard to the makeup of our modern world. It is separation on the basis of prejudice that is to be deplored, not the great diversity that can and should occur among the churches as they uniquely reach out to those whom the Holy Spirit has gifted and impassioned them to reach.

18. From a marketplace perspective, see Richard Whiteley and Diane Hessan, *Customer Centered Growth* (Reading, Mass.: Addison-Wesley, 1996), 22.

19. There are many other ways to discuss targeting whom it is you are trying to reach, such as focusing on particular segments within the population in light of geography, demographics, or culture. I believe that the targeting I have outlined is both biblical and appropriate. A good introduction to this can be found in Warren, *Purpose Driven Church*, 155–84.

20. Source unknown.

21. On the theological issues related to such rebaptisms, see the author's "Rebaptism in the Life of the Church," *Search* 19, no. 2 (winter 1989): 24–33.

22. See "A Study of Adults Baptized in Southern Baptist Churches, 1993," conducted by the Home Mission Board Research Division of the Southern Baptist Convention in conjunction with the Home Mission Board Evangelism Section as reported in the *Biblical Recorder* 161, no. 15 (15 April 1995): 12.

23. "Does Evangelism Have a Future in America?" *NetFax/The Leadership Network*, no. 32 (13 November 1995).

24. The true mark of a changed life, of course, is the fruit of the Spirit as detailed in the fifth chapter of Galatians.

25. An excellent discussion of gauging success in this fashion can be found in Hybels, *Rediscovering Church*, 195–201.

Chapter 2: Rethinking Evangelism

1. See David Ricks, *Big Business Blunders: Mistakes in Multi-National Marketing* (Homewood, Ill.: Dow Jones-Irwin, 1983).

2. Doug Smith, "Know a Culture; Boost Bottom Line," *The Charlotte Observer*, 21 May 1996, D1.

3. Quoted in Allan Cox, with Julie Liesse, *Redefining Corporate Soul: Linking Purpose and People* (Chicago: Irwin, 1996), 91.

4. Some of the thoughts in this section were first introduced and have been adapted from the author's contribution to David S. Dockery, ed., *The Challenge of Postmodernism*, 2d ed. (Grand Rapids: Bridgepoint/Baker, 2001).

5. For excellent introductions into the life and mind of the unchurched, see George Barna's latest survey material at www.barna.org. Note also the following works, which, while some might be dated by the 1990s, reveal the basic dispositions of the unchurched that often remain timeless: Phillip L. Berman, *The Search for Meaning: Americans Talk about What They Believe and Why* (New York: Ballantine, 1990); William D. Hendricks, *Exit Interviews: Revealing Stories of Why People Are Leaving the Church* (Chicago: Moody, 1993); Thom S. Rainer, *Surprising Insights from the Unchurched* (Grand Rapids: Zondervan, 2001); Wade Clark Roof, *A Generation of Seekers* (San Francisco: Harper & Row, 1993) and *Spiritual Marketplace: Baby Boomers and the Remaking of American Religion* (Princeton: Princeton University Press, 1999); Lee Strobel, *Inside the Mind of Unchurched Harry: Why People Steer Clear of God and the Church and How You Can Respond* (Grand Rapids: Zondervan, 1993).

6. For a detailed discussion of Hunter's ten characteristics of secular people, see the first chapter of his book *How to Reach Secular People* (Nashville: Abingdon, 1992).

7. See Andres Tapia, "Reaching the First Post-Christian Generation," *Christianity Today*, 12 September 1994, 18. On postmodernism, see Dockery, *Challenge of Postmodernism;* and Gene Edward Veith Jr., *Postmodern Times: A Christian Guide to Contemporary Thought and Culture* (Wheaton: Crossway, 1994). The best introduction, however, is Stanley Grenz, *A Primer on Postmodernism* (Grand Rapids: Eerdmans, 1995). For more on the attitudes of Baby Busters, see Lawrence J. Bradford and Claire Raines, *Twenty-Something: Managing and Motivating Today's New Work Force* (New York: Master Media Ltd., 1992); Tim Celek and Dieter Zander, *Inside the Soul of a New Generation: Insights and Strategies for Reaching Busters* (Grand Rapids: Zondervan, 1996); Kevin Graham Ford, *Jesus for a New Generation: Putting the Gospel in the Language of Xers* (Downers Grove, Ill.: InterVarsity Press,

1995); and Karen Ritchie, *Marketing to Generation X* (New York: Lexington Books, 1995).

8. Barna, *State of the Church 2002*, 55.

9. Barna, *Virtual America*, 82. In January of 2000, 38 percent of the American population believed that absolute moral truth exists. In November of 2001 that number dropped to only 22 percent. See www.barna.org.

10. Barna, *State of the Church 2002*, 70.

11. Barna, *Index of Leading Spiritual Indicators*, 77–78.

12. Ibid., 79.

13. James T. Patterson and Peter Kim, *America Told the Truth* (New York: Dutton Plume, 1992), 28.

14. George Barna, *The Barna Report 1992–1993* (Ventura, Calif.: Regal, 1992), 61. Only 23 percent of the population rated the image of the Roman Catholic Church as "very favorable."

15. Robert Bellah et al., *Habits of the Heart: Individualism and Commitment in American Life* (San Francisco: Harper & Row, 1985), 221.

16. A case in point can be evidenced by my own denomination, the Southern Baptist Convention, which strongly encourages its churches to organize its evangelism through the Sunday school. The result has been several years of declining baptisms, and seven out of every ten churches having plateaued or declined in membership and attendance. One cannot help but link a denomination's growth record with its chosen method of evangelism.

17. Adapted from Gordon Aeschliman, *Cages of Pain: Healing for Disillusioned Christians* (Dallas: Word, 1991), 24–26.

18. Both Kristina and her roommate gave Christianity a second chance, came to the church I pastor, and gave their lives to Christ. Kristina is now a member of our staff. She gave me permission to tell her story.

19. A previous book by the author, *Opening the Front Door: Worship and Church Growth* (Nashville: Convention Press, 1992), essentially puts forth a contemporary, seeker-sensitive model of worship. One of the best models for such an environment would be the Saddleback Valley Community Church. On Saddleback, see Warren, *Purpose Driven Church*.

20. Every barrier, that is, except the scandal of the cross. One of the myths of a seeker-targeted environment is that there is an abandonment of orthodoxy in an effort to cater to the sensibilities of the seeker. This is a caricature and does not reflect the vast majority of seeker-targeted churches.

21. The author's own church, Mecklenburg Community Church, falls into this category. The best-known example, however, is Willow Creek Community Church in South Barrington, Illinois. On Willow Creek, see Hybels, *Rediscovering Church*.

22. George Barna, *Evangelism That Works* (Ventura, Calif.: Regal, 1995), 40.

23. Strobel, *Unchurched Harry*, 85–91.

24. Barna, *Evangelism That Works*, 130.

25. On the Bible's emphasis on this approach, see Matthew 28:18–20; Acts 1:8; 6:7–8, 10; 8:4–8, 26–35; 9:10–18; 11:19–21; 1 Peter 3:15.

26. One of the best books for effective communication to the contemporary seeker is by Bill Hybels and Mark Mittelberg, *Becoming a Contagious Christian* (Grand Rapids: Zondervan, 1994), along with Rick Richardson's *Evangelism Outside the Box* (Downers Grove, Ill.: InterVarsity Press, 2000). See also the updated version of Paul Little's *How to Give Away Your Faith* (Downers Grove, Ill.: InterVarsity Press, 1988). On sharing within the confines of a relationship, see also Joseph C. Aldrich, *Life-Style Evangelism* (Portland, Ore.: Multnomah, 1981); and Jim Petersen, *Living Proof* (Colorado Springs: NavPress, 1989).

27. Chip Walker, "Word of Mouth," *American Demographics* 17, no. 7 (July 1995): 38–45.

28. Barna, *Evangelism That Works*, 72.

29. Michael Green, *Evangelism in the Early Church* (Grand Rapids: Eerdmans, 1970), 173.

30. Barna, *State of the Church 2002*, 36.

31. Excerpted from Ken Garfield, "Graham in Charlotte: Not Your Father's Crusade," *The Charlotte Observer*, 20 March 1996, 1C.

32. Ibid.

33. G. A. Pritchard, *Willow Creek Seeker Services: Evaluating a New Way of Doing Church* (Grand Rapids: Baker, 1996), 189.

34. Barna, *Evangelism That Works*, 87.

35. On services designed with the seeker in mind, see Ed Dobson, *Starting a Seeker Sensitive Service* (Grand Rapids: Zondervan, 1993); Hybels, *Rediscovering Church*, 28–32, 41–42, 167–81; Warren, *Purpose Driven Church*, 239–306; Pritchard, *Willow Creek Seeker Services;* and Sally Morgenthaler, *Worship Evangelism: Inviting Unbelievers into the Presence of God* (Grand Rapids: Zondervan, 1995).

36. Hybels and Mittelberg, *Contagious Christian*, 207.

Chapter 3: Rethinking Discipleship

1. Adapted from a message delivered by John Ortberg at Willow Creek Community Church, June 1994, Tape WCAIC120.

2. Bill Hull, *The Disciple-Making Pastor* (Old Tappan, N.J.: Revell, 1988), 13.

3. Another reason for this belief, but one outside the scope of this discussion, is the emphasis on decisionism throughout the history of American Christianity. Success in church and parachurch organizations has often been gauged by the number of professions of faith. As a result, once someone makes a decision for Christ, church members feel the church's mission has been accomplished.

4. Detailing the decline of discipleship in the life of the contemporary church is beyond the scope of this book. An introduction can be found in Thom and Joani Schultz, *Why Nobody Learns Much of Anything at Church: And How to Fix It* (Loveland, Colo.: Group, 1993).

5. George Barna, *Ministry Currents* 1, no. 4 (October/December 1991): 9.

6. C. S. Lewis, *The Screwtape Letters* (New York: Bantam, 1982), 4.

7. After his conversion, Paul went from Damascus to Arabia and then returned to Damascus (Gal. 1:16). Most believe he went away to reflect on his decision and to commune with God. Scholars such as F. F. Bruce suggest that Paul's postconversion preaching in the synagogues of Damascus followed this journey and that his trip to Jerusalem to be introduced to the leaders of the church occurred a full three years after his conversion. On this, see F. F. Bruce, *Paul: Apostle of the Heart Set Free* (Grand Rapids: Eerdmans, 1977), 74–82.

8. Eugene Peterson, *A Long Obedience in the Same Direction* (Downers Grove, Ill.: InterVarsity Press, 1980).

9. Barna, *Index of Leading Spiritual Indicators*, 77.

10. This analogy is a contemporized version from one given by Dallas Willard in *The Spirit of the Disciplines: Understanding How God Changes Lives* (San Francisco: Harper & Row, 1988), 3–4.

11. On this, see Willard, *Spirit of the Disciplines;* and Richard Foster, *The Celebration of Discipline* (San Francisco: Harper & Row, 1978).

12. There are numerous examples of how various churches have fleshed this out. Two excellent models can be found in Warren, *Purpose Driven Church*, 343–92; and Hybels, *Rediscovering Church*, 167–82. See also Alexander B. Bruce, *Training of the Twelve* (Grand Rapids: Kregel, 1971); and Bill Hull, *Disciple-Making Pastor.*

13. Hybels, *Rediscovering Church*, 191.

14. Bill Donahue and Russ Robinson, *Building a Church of Small Groups* (Grand Rapids: Zondervan/Willow Creek Association, 2001), 38–43.

15. Ibid., 178.

16. One of the best introductions to small groups is found in Gareth Weldon Icenogle, *Biblical Foundations for Small Group Ministry* (Downers Grove, Ill.: InterVarsity Press, 1994).

17. Thom Rainer, *Giant Awakenings* (Nashville: Broadman and Holman, 1995), 58. Unfortunately, many churches have not engaged in any type of adaptation and, as a result, are experiencing plateauing or declining Sunday school programs.

18. Works that support the continued use of Sunday school but agree that it is in need of rethinking include Ken Hemphill, *Revitalizing the Sunday Morning Dinosaur* (Nashville: Broadman and Holman, 1996); Bill Taylor, *21 Truths, Traditions, and Trends: Propelling the Sunday School into the 21st Century* (Nashville: Convention Press, 1996); and Elmer L. Towns, *10 Sunday Schools That Dared to Change* (Ventura, Calif.: Regal, 1993).

19. On strategic discipleship relationships, see Paul Stanley and Robert Clinton, *Connecting: The Mentoring Relationships You Need to Succeed in Life* (Colorado Springs: NavPress, 1992); Ted W. Engstrom, *The Fine Art of Mentoring: Passing On to Others What God Has Given to You* (Brentwood, Tenn.: Wolgemuth and Hyatt, 1989); Bobb Biehl, *Mentoring: Confidence in Finding*

a Mentor and Becoming One (Nashville: Broadman and Holman, 1996); and David Simpson, *It's Who You Know: Winning with People* (Gresham, Ore.: Vision House, 1995).

20. On adding different types of small groups to an existing Sunday school, see Michael C. Mack, *The Synergy Church: A Strategy for Integrating Small Groups and Sunday School* (Grand Rapids: Baker, 1996).

21. An excellent introduction to small group ministry can be found in Donahue and Robinson's *Building a Church of Small Groups*.

Chapter 4: Rethinking Ministry

1. Adapted from Bill Hybels, *Honest to God* (Grand Rapids: Zondervan, 1990), 107–9.

2. Barna, *State of the Church 2002*, 22.

3. From the Springfield, Oregon, Public Schools Newsletter, as printed in Charles Swindoll, *Growing Strong in the Seasons of Life* (Portland, Ore.: Multnomah, 1983), 312.

4. For an excellent book on this subject, see Greg Ogden, *The New Reformation: Restoring the Ministry to the People of God* (Grand Rapids: Zondervan, 1990). See also Ray C. Stedman, *Body Life*, rev. ed. (Grand Rapids: Discovery House, 1995); and Frank R. Tillapaugh, *Unleashing the Church* (Ventura, Calif.: Regal, 1982).

5. Hybels, *Honest to God*, 115.

6. Barna, *Index of Leading Spiritual Indicators*, 66.

7. There are many tools that assist churches in the development of this process. My personal favorite is Networking, developed by Willow Creek Community Church and distributed through Willow Creek Resources/Zondervan. Not only does it involve a testing process for spiritual gifts, but it includes the important dynamics of passion and temperament type as well. For a conceptual overview of this approach, see Bruce Bugbee, *What You Do Best in the Body of Christ: Discover Your Spiritual Gifts, Personal Style, and God-Given Passion* (Grand Rapids: Zondervan, 1995).

8. James C. Collins and Jerry I. Porras, *Built to Last: Successful Habits of Visionary Companies* (New York: HarperBusiness, 1994), 140–68.

9. Ibid., 146.

Chapter 5: Rethinking Worship

1. For a more detailed understanding of the nature, theology, and history of Christian worship, see Ralph Martin, *The Worship of God* (Grand Rapids: Eerdmans, 1982); and James F. White, *Introduction to Christian Worship*, rev. ed. (Nashville: Abingdon, 1990). On the dynamics of Christian worship, see Robert Webber, *Worship Is a Verb* (Waco: Word, 1985).

2. Leith Anderson, *Dying for Change: An Arresting Look at the New Realities Confronting Churches and Para-Church Ministries* (Minneapolis: Bethany, 1990), 13.

3. Robert E. Logan, *Beyond Church Growth: Action Plans for Developing a Dynamic Church* (Old Tappan, N.J.: Revell, 1989), 60.

4. As reported in "News and Notes," *The Charlotte Observer,* 9 March 1996, 2G. It is interesting to note that similarly 59 percent of clergy believed their Lutheran church is friendly, compared with only 35 percent of those in the pews.

5. Barna, *Index of Leading Spiritual Indicators,* 50.

6. According to the research of George Barna, as reported by Terri Jo Ryan, "Survey finds many Christians don't understand worship," *Waco Tribune-Herald,* as found online at WacoTrib.com.

7. Herb Miller, *How to Build a Magnetic Church,* Creative Leadership Series, ed. Lyle E. Schaller (Nashville: Abingdon, 1987), 55.

8. On this, see the author's *Opening the Front Door: Worship and Church Growth* (Nashville: Convention Press, 1992).

9. Figures supporting this can be found in the author's *Opening the Front Door,* 16–19. Such figures are reported annually through the Church Uniform Letter of Southern Baptist Churches as compiled by the Baptist Sunday School Board, giving an excellent basis for tracking this shift.

10. Barna, *State of the Church 2002,* 32.

11. Kennon L. Callahan, *Twelve Keys to an Effective Church* (San Francisco: Harper & Row, 1983), 24.

12. Warren, *Purpose Driven Church,* 241. See also Morgenthaler, *Worship Evangelism.*

13. As Ronald Allen and Gordon Borror have noted, "Sometimes we . . . try to build moral/theological fences to defend our taste." See Ronald Allen and Gordon Borror, *Worship: Rediscovering the Missing Jewel* (Portland, Ore.: Multnomah, 1982), 166.

14. These two terms have taken quite a beating in recent years from certain quarters of the Christian world. Rather than use less pejorative terms, I've decided to maintain their use. When carefully defined, they can help us constructively rethink worship in the church.

15. As mentioned in chapter 2, certain churches have developed seeker services that are completely designed to present the gospel to non-Christians. When seeker sensitivity reaches this level, it is best termed a seeker service, and worship for the believer should then be offered through another service.

16. Anderson, *Dying for Change,* 43.

17. Doug Murren, *The Baby Boomerang: Catching Baby Boomers as They Return to Church* (Ventura, Calif.: Regal, 1990), 188.

18. Warren, *Purpose Driven Church,* 283.

19. Harry Lucenay, "Blending the Traditional and Contemporary," in Joe R. Stacker and Wesley Forbis, eds., *Authentic Worship: Exalting God and Reaching People* (Nashville: Convention Press, 1990), 22.

20. Warren, *Purpose Driven Church,* 283.

21. Adapted from Mark Wingfield, "Music Doesn't Change," Associated Baptist Press, as published in *The Biblical Recorder*, 165, no. 43 (18 December 1999): 1.

22. Morgenthaler, *Worship Evangelism*, 128.

23. On this, see Colleen Carroll, *The New Faithful: Why Young Adults Are Embracing Christian Orthodoxy* (Chicago: Loyola Press, 2002); Robert Webber, *Ancient-Future Faith: Rethinking Evangelicalism for a Postmodern World* (Grand Rapids: Baker, 1999).

24. This information is based on the research of Dr. George Hunter, Dean of Asbury Seminary's School of World Mission, as recorded in *The Win Arn Growth Report*, no. 33, 2.

25. Karen L. Willoughby, "Research Shows Nine Trends in Evangelistic Services," *Baptist Press*, 14 June 1996. The article was based on the research of Thom Rainer, released in the book *Effective Evangelistic Churches* (Nashville: Broadman and Holman, 1996). This research is particularly intriguing as the Southern Baptist Church has been so clearly marked by the traditional/revivalistic style of worship, which now, according to Rainer, constitutes only 40 percent of the most effective evangelistic churches in the SBC.

26. Marva J. Dawn, *Reaching Out without Dumbing Down: A Theology of Worship for the Turn-of-the-Century Culture* (Grand Rapids: Eerdmans, 1995).

27. In essence, a postmodern, post-Christian world is one in which all the foundations, such as truth and morality, have been removed. For a good introduction to postmodern thought and culture, see Gene Edward Veith Jr., *Postmodern Times: A Christian Guide to Contemporary Thought and Culture* (Wheaton: Crossway, 1994), along with Stanley Grenz's *A Primer on Postmodernism*, and David Dockery, ed., *The Challenge of Postmodernism: An Evangelical Engagement* (Grand Rapids: Baker, 2001), which contains an article by the author titled "Evangelism in a Postmodern World."

28. On the subject of truth in our modern world, see the author's *What Is Truth? A Comparative Study of the Positions of Cornelius Van Til, Francis Schaeffer, Carl F. H. Henry, Donald Bloesch, Millard Erickson* (Nashville: Broadman and Holman, 1994).

29. Kenneth A. Myers, *All God's Children and Blue Suede Shoes: Christians and Popular Culture* (Westchester, Ill.: Crossway, 1989), xii. Myers, formerly with National Public Radio, also produces an excellent bimonthly audio journal on Christianity and culture called The Mars Hill Tapes.

30. This seems to be the conviction of David Wells, *No Place for Truth* (Grand Rapids: Eerdmans, 1993). Wells's warnings are well taken, but they mistakenly intimate that any innovative methodology that borrows from the world of business or psychology, much less a contextualization that reflects the modern world, automatically necessitates compromise. His critiques are simply insufficiently nuanced. A much more balanced critique, yet still voicing many of the same concerns, can be found in Bruce and Marshall Shelley, *Consumer Church* (Downers Grove, Ill.: InterVarsity Press, 1992). An excellent volume to read alongside such works is Richard J. Mouw, *Consult-*

ing the Faithful: What Christian Intellectuals Can Learn from Popular Religion (Grand Rapids: Eerdmans, 1994).

31. Mouw, *Consulting the Faithful*, 8.

32. On this, see Robert G. Duffett, *A Relevant Word: Communicating the Gospel to Seekers* (Valley Forge, Pa.: Judson Press, 1995). For those familiar with H. Richard Niebuhr's categories, it is "Christ the Transformer of Culture," not "The Christ of Culture" or "Christ against Culture." On this, see H. Richard Niebuhr, *Christ and Culture* (New York: Harper & Row, 1951).

33. Charles H. Kraft, *Christianity in Culture* (Maryknoll, N.Y.: Orbis Books, 1979), 382.

34. Millard Erickson, *Christian Theology* (Grand Rapids: Baker, 1985), 113–16.

35. Charles Colson, with Ellen Santilli Vaughn, *The Body: Being Light in Darkness* (Dallas: Word, 1992), 48.

36. Donald P. Hustad, foreword to *People in the Presence of God: Models and Directions for Worship* by Barry Liesch (Grand Rapids: Zondervan, 1988), x.

37. Source unknown.

Chapter 6: Rethinking Structure

1. The story of Mother Teresa was adapted from Philip K. Howard, *The Death of Common Sense: How Law Is Suffocating America* (New York: Random House, 1994), 3–4.

2. On the importance and relevance of church structure to a changing world, see Howard Snyder, *The Problem of Wineskins: Church Structure in a Technological Age* (Downers Grove, Ill.: InterVarsity Press, 1975).

3. See Dean R. Spitzer, *Super-Motivation: A Blueprint for Energizing Your Organization from Top to Bottom* (New York: AMACOM, 1995), 43–58.

4. Geoffrey James, *Business Wisdom of the Electronic Elite* (New York: Random House, 1996), 99.

5. Michael Hammer, *Beyond Reengineering: How the Process-Centered Organization Is Changing Our Work and Our Lives* (New York: HarperBusiness, 1996), xii.

6. Ibid.

7. Ibid., 8.

8. James, *Business Wisdom of the Electronic Elite*, 53–54.

9. Ibid., 54.

10. George Barna, *User Friendly Churches* (Ventura, Calif.: Regal, 1991), 137.

11. Warren, *Purpose Driven Church*, 376.

12. Bill Hull, *Can We Save the Evangelical Church?* (Grand Rapids: Revell, 1993), 102.

13. Warren, *Purpose Driven Church*, 376.

14. Ibid., 366–67.

15. Howard, *Death of Common Sense*, 11.

16. Ibid., 68.
17. Ibid., 60.
18. Ibid., 64–65.
19. Ibid., 65.
20. Warren, *Purpose Driven Church*, 377.
21. Barna, *User Friendly Churches*, 141.
22. See Howard, *Death of Common Sense*, 99.
23. See Allan Cox, with Julie Liesse, *Redefining Corporate Soul: Linking Purpose and People* (Chicago: Irwin, 1996), 69.
24. William Easum, *Sacred Cows Make Gourmet Burgers: Ministry Anytime, Anywhere, by Anybody* (Nashville: Abingdon, 1995), 55.
25. On the pastor as equipper and leader, see the author's "Why Pastors Must Be Leaders," *Leadership* 27, no. 4 (fall 1996): 48–53. On the pastor as leader, see Bill Hybels, *Courageous Leadership* (Grand Rapids: Zondervan/Willow Creek Association, 2002).
26. Warren, *Purpose Driven Church*, 376.
27. Easum, *Sacred Cows*, 51.
28. Ibid., 378.
29. One of the reasons why biblical leaders like Nehemiah were so effective was because they were team players. George Barna's research on effective churches has discovered that while the pastor in successful churches is usually a dominant leader, he is ultimately a team player. On this, see Barna, *User Friendly Churches*, 153.
30. Jon R. Katzenbach and Douglas K. Smith, *The Wisdom of Teams: Creating the High-Performance Organization* (Boston: Harvard Business School Press, 1993), 1. On the importance and value of teams, see also Don Martin, *TeamThink* (New York: Dutton, 1993).
31. On this, see Richard S. Wellins, William C. Byham, and Jeanne M. Wilson, *Empowered Teams: Creating Self-Directed Work Groups That Improve Quality, Productivity, and Participation* (San Francisco: Jossey-Bass, 1991).
32. Katzenbach and Smith, *Wisdom of Teams*, 18.
33. On this, see Hammer, *Beyond Reengineering*, 108–37.
34. Source unknown.
35. Adapted from a chapel address given by Fred Craddock at the Southern Baptist Theological Seminary, Louisville, Kentucky.

Chapter 7: Rethinking Community

1. Bill Wolfe, "Church Meeting Ends in Fray, Beleaguered Pastor Resigns Amid Turmoil," *The Courier-Journal*, 10 December 1990, 1A.
2. See the Barna study on why people do not go to church, cited in the introduction, which revealed that 61 percent did not attend because there were "too many problems" in the church.
3. Adapted from Hybels, *Rediscovering Church*, 159.
4. Ibid.

5. C. S. Lewis, *The Four Loves* (New York: Harcourt Brace Jovanovich, 1960), 169.

6. Margery Williams, *The Velveteen Rabbit* (New York: Doubleday, 1958), 16–17.

7. Hybels, *Rediscovering Church*, 47.

8. Adapted from Robert Fulghum, *All I Really Need to Know I Learned in Kindergarten* (New York: Villard Books, 1989), 56–58.

9. Adapted from Leith Anderson, *A Church for the 21st Century* (Minneapolis: Bethany, 1992), 86.

10. Dietrich Bonhoeffer, *Life Together* (New York: Harper & Row, 1954), 20.

11. Philip B. Jones, "Smallness and Decline Typify Southern Baptist Churches," *Research Review* no. 6 (fall 1996): 1.

12. Bonhoeffer, *Life Together*, 26.

13. Warren Bennis and Patricia Ward Biederman, *Organizing Genius: The Secrets of Creative Collaboration* (Reading, Mass.: Addison-Wesley, 1997), 5–6.

14. Francis A. Schaeffer, "The Mark of the Christian," in *The Complete Works of Francis A. Schaeffer: A Christian Worldview*, vol. 4 (Westchester, Ill.: Crossway, 1982), 187–88.

Chapter 8: From Rethinking to Change

1. Compiled and adapted from the annual production of such reflections from the staff of Beloit College, Wisconsin, for those students who were born in 1980.

2. Some of the best books on this include John Kotter, *Leading Change* (Boston: Harvard Business School Press, 1996); Alan Nelson and Gene Appel, *How to Change Your Church (Without Killing It)* (Nashville: Word, 2000); and Jim Herrington, Mike Bonem, and James H. Furr, *Leading Congregational Change: A Practical Guide for the Transformational Journey* (San Francisco: Jossey-Bass, 2001). For a narrative of one church's journey, see Randy Frazee's *The Comeback Congregation: New Life for a Troubled Ministry* (Nashville: Abingdon Press, 1995).

3. On this, see Everett M. Rogers, *Diffusion of Innovations*, 4th ed. (New York: Free Press, 1995). The diagram has been adapted from p. 262.

4. Kotter, *Leading Change*, 36.

5. Ibid., 88–89.

6. Warren, *Purpose Driven Church*, 111.

7. As quoted by John Maxwell, *The 21 Irrefutable Laws of Leadership* (Nashville: Thomas Nelson, 1998), 28–29.

8. From Alan Loy McGinnis.

Conclusion

1. Warren, *Purpose Driven Church*, 59.

2. George Barna, *The Frog in the Kettle: What Christians Need to Know about Life in the Year 2000* (Ventura, Calif.: Regal, 1990), 21–22.

3. Peter Benson and Carolyn Elkin, *Effective Christian Education: A National Study of Protestant Congregations* (Minneapolis: Search Institute, 1990), 67.

4. "News and Notes," *The Charlotte Observer,* 23 March 1996, 2G.

5. Charles Trueheart, "Welcome to the Next Church," *The Atlantic Monthly* 278, no. 2 (August 1996): 46.

6. Gene Getz, *Sharpening the Focus of the Church* (Wheaton: Victor, 1984), 78–79.

7. Many critics of the contemporary church cite narcissism as a great concern, usually when addressing the issue of theological compromise by contemporary churches with a zeal to be user friendly. The fear is that a market-driven mentality will so invade the church that orthodoxy will be abandoned for the sake of warm bodies. When and if this ever were to take place, it would deserve a resounding condemnation. Fortunately, it is not an epidemic, and contrary to many pundits, the unchurched do not call for the abandonment of commitment, challenge, or orthodoxy when queried as to their wishes for the church. The greater manifestation of narcissism is within the mind-set of believers in regard to the purpose of the church, namely, that it exists to meet their needs.

8. Henri J. M. Nouwen, *The Return of the Prodigal Son: A Story of Homecoming* (New York: Continuum, 1995), 62.

9. Robert E. Coleman, *The Master Plan of Evangelism* (Old Tappan, N.J.: Revell, 1963), 101.

10. The story of Kerri Strug has been adapted from several sources, including Mark Starr, "Leap of Faith," *Newsweek,* 5 August 1996, 40–48; Ron Green, "The Ultimate Act of Courage," *The Charlotte Observer,* 24 July 1996, 1A, 12A; Liz Chandler, "Strug Vaults U.S.," *The Charlotte Observer,* 24 July 1996, 1B, 7B; and Liz Chandler, "Gymnast's Will to Win at All Cost Questioned," *The Charlotte Observer,* 25 July 1996, 1A, 3A.

11. Adapted from Tony Campolo's use of the story in *Who Switched the Price Tags?* (Waco: Word, 1986), 170–71.

Select Bibliography

Anderson, Leith. *Dying for Change: An Arresting Look at the New Realities Confronting Churches and Para-Church Ministries.* Minneapolis: Bethany, 1990.

Barna, George. *Evangelism That Works.* Ventura, Calif.: Regal, 1995.

_____. *User Friendly Churches: What Successful Churches Have in Common and Why Their Ideas Work.* Ventura, Calif.: Regal, 1991.

Bilezikian, Gilbert. *Community 101: Reclaiming the Local Church as Community of Oneness.* Grand Rapids: Zondervan/Willow Creek Association, 1997.

Collins, James C., and Jerry I. Porras. *Built to Last: Successful Habits of Visionary Companies.* New York: HarperBusiness, 1994.

_____. *Good to Great: Why Some Companies Make the Leap . . . and Others Don't.* New York: HarperBusiness, 2001.

Cordeiro, Wayne. *Doing Church as a Team.* Ventura, Calif.: Regal, 2001.

Donahue, Bill, and Russ Robinson. *Building a Church of Small Groups.* Grand Rapids: Zondervan/Willow Creek Association, 2001.

Frazee, Randy, with Lyle Schaller. *The Comeback Congregation: New Life for a Troubled Ministry.* Nashville: Abingdon, 1995.

Getz, Gene. *Sharpening the Focus of the Church.* Wheaton: Victor, 1984.

Gibbs, Eddie. *ChurchNext: Quantum Changes in How We Do Ministry.* Downers Grove, Ill.: InterVarsity Press, 2000.

Hammer, Michael, and James Champy. *Reengineering the Corporation: A Manifesto for Business Revolution.* New York: HarperBusiness, 1993.

Hull, Bill. *Can We Save the Evangelical Church?* Grand Rapids: Revell, 1993.

Hunter, George G., III. *Church for the Unchurched.* Nashville: Abingdon, 1996.

Hybels, Bill. *Courageous Leadership.* Grand Rapids: Zondervan/Willow Creek Association, 2002.

Hybels, Bill, and Mark Mittelberg. *Becoming a Contagious Christian.* Grand Rapids: Zondervan, 1994.

Hybels, Lynne, and Bill Hybels. *Rediscovering Church.* Grand Rapids: Zondervan, 1995.

Kotter, John P. *Leading Change.* Boston: Harvard Business School Press, 1996.

Maxwell, John. *The 21 Irrefutable Laws of Leadership.* Nashville: Thomas Nelson, 1998.

Mittelberg, Mark. *Building a Contagious Church.* Grand Rapids: Zondervan/Willow Creek Association, 2000.

Morgenthaler, Sally. *Worship Evangelism: Inviting Unbelievers into the Presence of God.* Grand Rapids: Zondervan, 1995.

Mouw, Richard J. *Consulting the Faithful: What Christian Intellectuals Can Learn from Popular Religion.* Grand Rapids: Eerdmans, 1994.

Nelson, Alan, and Gene Appel. *How to Change Your Church (Without Killing It).* Nashville: Word, 2000.

Ogden, Greg. *The New Reformation: Restoring the Ministry to the People of God.* Grand Rapids: Zondervan, 1990.

Pine, Joseph, and James H. Gilmore. *The Experience Economy: Work Is Theatre and Every Business a Stage.* Boston: Harvard Business School Press, 1999.

Rainer, Thom. *Surprising Insights from the Unchurched and Proven Ways to Reach Them.* Grand Rapids: Zondervan, 2001.

Regele, Mike, with Mark Schulz. *Death of the Church*. Grand Rapids: Zondervan, 1995.

Richardson, Rick. *Evangelism Outside the Box: New Ways to Help People Experience the Good News*. Downers Grove, Ill.: InterVarsity Press, 2000.

Russell, Bob, with Rusty Russell. *When God Builds a Church: 10 Principles for Growing a Dynamic Church*. West Monroe, La.: Howard, 2000.

Schultz, Thom, and Joani Schultz. *Why Nobody Learns Much of Anything at Church: And How to Fix It*. Loveland, Colo.: Group, 1993.

Stanley, Andy, and Ed Young. *Can We Do That? 24 Innovative Practices That Will Change the Way You Do Church*. West Monroe, La.: Howard, 2002.

Strobel, Lee. *Inside the Mind of Unchurched Harry: Why People Steer Clear of God and the Church and How You Can Respond*. Grand Rapids: Zondervan, 1993.

Warren, Rick. *The Purpose Driven Church*. Grand Rapids: Zondervan, 1995.

James Emery White is the founding and senior pastor of Mecklenburg Community Church in Charlotte, North Carolina. Dr. White holds M.Div. and Ph.D. degrees from Southern Seminary and has completed advanced graduate study at Vanderbilt University and continuing education at the University of Oxford, England. He is also an adjunct professor of Theology and Culture at Gordon-Conwell Theological Seminary. The author of several books, including *A Search for the Spiritual, Life-Defining Moments,* and *Long Night's Journey into Day,* he and his wife, Susan, live in Charlotte with their four children.

For more information on Mecklenburg Community Church, including resources and conferences for churches and church leaders, visit www.mecklenburg.org.